MAGIC
IN THE
LANDSCAPE

"More often than not, modern humans have stumbled obliviously and deleteriously across the landscape they inhabit. Accordingly, their perception of reality has become ever more shallow, superficial, and desacralized—or, worst of all, may now be abandoned entirely in favor of virtual simulacra. Swimming against this tide for over half a century, Nigel Pennick is a tireless explorer and surveyor of the ensouled and eldritch world that still persists around us, despite our blind and clumsy attempts to constantly 'develop' and smother it for short-term gains. At its root, *Magic in the Landscape* is a treatise about the authenticity that results from meaningful human interaction with the earth and its myriad energies. In this modest 'spiritual gazetteer,' Pennick reveals some of the countless crossroads where local traditions and topography intersect, always with the aim of shedding light upon the deeper soulscape that these practices reflect."

MICHAEL MOYNIHAN, PH.D., COEDITOR OF
TYR: MYTH—CULTURE—TRADITION

"In this book, Nigel expertly weaves together a narrative exploring the power of place and humankind's changing relationship with it. It is a thought-provoking and well-written exploration of the physical and spiritual aspects of the landscape, revealing the world about us to be more than an impersonal backdrop against which we live out our lives. Within these pages, Nigel reminds us of the importance of how we choose to orient ourselves within this ensouled world and of the necessity for discernment in any mundane and magical interactions we might make with the land beneath our heels."

MARTIN DUFFY, AUTHOR OF
*THE SPIRIT OF THE DOWNS:
WITCHCRAFT AND MAGIC IN SUSSEX*

"In this book, Pennick does what he does so well—wears his deep learning lightly and makes more profound and highly readable connections between magic and the visible world than you could shake a geomantic staff at. He reminds us of the necessity of sacred space and the disenchantment of the world, demolishing the prettification of rural Britain and our loss of magical tradition. He also shows that what we now call feng shui existed in Britain long before it got fashionable and that just a few centuries ago major buildings were founded at times and places indicated by astrology. Should we need such a reminder, a postscript on magic makes it clear that Pennick is not some tenured academic toeing the scientism party line but a practicing magician who is writing from real personal experience."

DAVID LEE, AUTHOR OF
*LIFE FORCE: SENSED ENERGY IN BREATHWORK,
PSYCHEDELIA AND CHAOS MAGIC*

MAGIC
IN THE
LANDSCAPE

EARTH MYSTERIES & GEOMANCY

NIGEL PENNICK

Destiny Books
Rochester, Vermont

Destiny Books
One Park Street
Rochester, Vermont 05767
www.DestinyBooks.com

Text stock is SFI certified

Destiny Books is a division of Inner Traditions International

All photographs and illustrations are by the author. Artifacts in Nigel Pennick's collection and archive engravings courtesy of the Library of the European Tradition.

Originally published in the United Kingdom in 2013 by Lear Books under the title *Magic in the Landscape*

Cataloging-in-Publication Data for this title is available from the Library of Congress

ISBN 978-1-62055-879-9 (print)
ISBN 978-1-62055-880-5 (ebook)

Printed and bound in the United States by Lake Book Manufacturing, Inc. The text stock is SFI certified. The Sustainable Forestry Initiative® program promotes sustainable forest management.

10 9 8 7 6 5 4 3 2 1

Text design and layout by Priscilla Baker
This book was typeset in Garamond Premier Pro with Kiona, Gill Sans, and Snell Roundhand used as display typefaces

To send correspondence to the author of this book, mail a first-class letter to the author c/o Inner Traditions • Bear & Company, One Park Street, Rochester, VT 05767, and we will forward the communication.

CONTENTS

☉∕☉

INTRODUCTION

A VANISHING WORLD IN NEED OF RESCUE

Many writings about historical subjects attempt to reconstruct the past by creating a depiction of an ideal time when the writer perceives that the system under study was perfect or intact. All history is a kind of editing; we are presented with records, stories, and opinions from the past from which we must try to construct some coherent narrative. The nature of events and how they are remembered, recorded, and transmitted is an uncertain territory. Time is a continuum, and we are present in it at a certain place. There is no generic moment: every incident that occurred was a real one, and every action happened at a particular time at a particular place. What has come before is only present as physical fragments, written and recorded documentation, legendary readings of events, stories handed down, and attempted reconstructions that seek to create an ambience of a historical period. Museums, reconstructions, and reenactments exist in the present: they are inevitably selective and creative works of the present that seek to present us with the illusion of being in the past—which we are not. Their many failings and falsifications are apparent wherever they take place.

The academic discipline of folklore and studies into earth mysteries, paganism, witchcraft, and magic are equally subject to this selection. Recorded evidence of much of the subject matter is extremely fragmentary and subject to widely varying interpretations. These

Fig. I.1. Spiral stone, Newgrange, Ireland

interpretations frequently present themselves as composing a self-contained system that ignores variations of individuals and of time. A simplified, homogenized, and idealized principle is presented as if it were the complex and irreducible reality. An indeterminate and imaginary period—"the past"—is often presented as a mythologized existence comparable to the dreamtime of the native Australian mythos. This is not a historical time and date like that of a recorded event, such as, for example, the laying of the foundation stone of Sir Christopher Wren's Saint Paul's Cathedral in London at 6:30 a.m. local apparent time, June 26 (Old Style), 1675, but rather is an idealized otherworldly time that remains forever in the eternal present in people's culture.

Religions based on supposed actual events treat them in this idealized way. In Christian iconography Jesus is always on the cross, and the actual and precise location, time, date, and duration of the crucifixion is unknown and has no importance to the mythos. But if it occurred, it was on a particular date, at a particular time, with a particular duration, after which the event was over. This event has been transferred into an eternal imaginary time. Those who take visitors around historic sites often say something like, "They would have sat here," a false way of viewing the past. There is no "would have": either someone did something at a specific time or they did not. "Would have" is the language of imaginary time, the fabrication of a story that masquerades as past reality.

Every person lumped under the various categories was, like you and me, an individual who lived for a particular time after his or her birth, which took place at a particular moment, as did his or her death. They were individuals born into particular families at particular places. They were taught by other individuals, each with their own histories and their own life stories. Most of these people are unknown; their life stories are lost, and we are lucky to have a few names and the occasional anecdote of one of their actions. Although writers, statisticians, and politicians talk as if there are real entities like "the British people," "witches," "ploughmen,"* "drivers," "criminals," "police officers," "foreigners," or "magicians," in actuality these categories tell us nothing about the character and lives of the individuals so categorized. Equally, the modes of study and their development and changes have their own history. Opinions commonly held as true in 1862 may have been discredited by 1912, revised in 1962, and overthrown by 2012, and they may be reinstated by 2062. During the periods when they held sway, these opinions were the norm, the orthodoxy, and one risked criticism or the loss of one's credibility or even one's career or life to claim another opinion. In folklore and wider historical reconstruction attempts, their history as subjects embeds within them the processes of their development. Many of the early investigators were

---

*Because the proper names for the play *The Plough and the Stars* and some song titles mentioned in this book use the British spelling of the word *plow*, the British spelling has been retained for this word and its variations in all instances. All other words with alternate British spellings have been Americanized.

driven by a wish to find customs and traditions that were unique to particular places—or at least what they then perceived to be unique—and that they saw as in danger of being lost. When an art has seemed threatened, then collecting has intensified so that people can record what was viewed as a vanishing world in need of rescue.

A nationalist agenda was present in many folklorists, and their success in identifying what they saw as national differences remains today. Hence the largely artificial divisions identifying folk art and traditional music played in the British Isles and the different versions of the styles in Canada and the United States. There are contemporary folk musicians who will only play what they consider to be Irish, English, or Scottish music, even though the standard repertoires of these three divisions contain a not-inconsiderable number of the same tunes. It is known that "Flowers of Edinburgh" has been played by traditional musicians in Cambridge since at least the middle of the nineteenth century; "The Glasgow Hornpipe" and "The Sheffield Apprentice" appear in the standard Irish repertoire, and there are many more examples of this.

Much heated sectarian and nationalist anger has been expended on arguments over the origins and ownership of traditional tunes. It is not easy to define a tune as belonging to a particular nation once we look at its origins and history, even if we know them. For example, is the ska song about an underground railway line in London, "All Change on the Bakerloo Line," Jamaican or English? Both. A modern instance of the nationalization of a song is "The Leaving of Liverpool," which was collected from an American singer in New York and which is about a port in England, yet because it was part of the repertoire of the Dubliners, an Irish group, it is now an "Irish" song.

The attempts to identify cultural artifacts that demonstrate national differences actually have gone a long way to creating differences that may not have existed before in such clearly defined ways. The very act of defining something as national—nationalizing what was once common property—is an act of political power-making intended to serve a political agenda. Making and publishing collections of music and other traditional performances defined national culture through the terms of what the collectors selected from what they found; items they deemed foreign or inappropriate were edited out, even though they were present among the musicians who played that music. The principle of selective amnesia is often an integral part of writing histories.

A similar process can be detected in certain areas of esoteric study, where practices that the collectors considered to be foreign or alien did not enter the record or were later forgotten. For example, the concept of feng shui was embedded within English landscape gardening in the eighteenth century to the point that its elements were taken for granted a century later and were all but unrecognized by the time that practitioners of new age ideas made feng shui fashionable again in the late twentieth century. When they brought it back, it was full-on Chinese in appearance, so nobody noticed the feng shui in the design of their local town park, what the Germans call "the English garden." Similarly, the influences of magic from various parts of the world in recorded traditional British witchcraft are scarcely noticed. Even in Wicca, the Malayan elements incorporated into the system by Gerald Brosseau Gardner* are assumed by many to originate in ancient Britain.

Every kind of human culture is syncretic in this way. The illusion of primal purity is a projection back on a mythic past, and often it is merely a device used by individuals and groups to gain power and control. As with everything in this transient world, human culture is ever changing, and its only manifestation is in the performance of its traditions. All living cultural traditions, wherever they are, are in a state of continuous evolution, adapting themselves to the particular conditions prevailing at the moment. The present moment is the result of what has preceded it, that intangible phenomenon that we call the past. What

---

*Gerald Brosseau Gardner (1884–1964) was an English Wiccan as well as an author and an amateur anthropologist and archaeologist.

humans have decided to call the "natural laws" of physics, the given nature of the materials with which we must work, and the culturally transmitted techniques of working with them, along with the social expectations of the moment, are engaged with by the performer, who must manage them with skill to produce the desired result. We cannot remove ourselves from the logic of the situation. It is an immutable condition from which we must work.

THE BRITISH RURAL LANDSCAPE

A Brief History

Your portion, make the best of it.
The landlords have the rest of it.

CYNICUS (MARTIN ANDERSON)

The countryside is often portrayed in the imagination as a rural idyll of pastoral peace and tranquillity. But this, even if desirable, is not a real understanding of true conditions, either historical or contemporary. The rural landscape we experience now is the current—and changing— result of a history of significant transformative influences that resulted in progressive urbanization, which continues today. The condition of the landscape as we experience it embeds events that altered it from a land where people worked it and much was held in common to one where private ownership became the norm. That had come about as the result of a pastoral culture that cultivated the land, transforming it from forest and wilderness into fields and gardens, much of which was in common ownership—common land.

The most significant element in the transformation, which has led to the present situation, was the enclosure of the common land. The ruling class decided that it had the power to take the land that was held in common by the lower class and use it to profit the few. Because Parliament was the preserve of the rich (and I write this when old-school-tie millionaires compose the higher echelons of the government), members who were used to voting through laws for their own profit decided to have an Act of Parliament that took away most of the common land from the peasantry. The king gladly signed it into law, for he too was to profit from this one-sided act of privatization. The land taken in this way was "improved" by the new owners with new agricultural techniques. Ancient footpaths and trackways were barred and ploughed up. Standing stones, upright monuments that may have been erected as far back as the Neolithic period, were uprooted, carted away, and broken up for road stone. Sacred trees that stood in the way of the

Fig. 1.1. Shropshire Fields, England

plough were felled. In Scotland this "improvement" took the form of the Highland Clearances, under which the peasant class was forcibly evicted from the land by the Scots lairds and forced to flee as refugees to other parts of Britain and, most notably, to Canada. In Scotland humans were replaced by more profitable sheep.

The suffering of those evicted from their own land was considered a price well worth paying by those who made a handsome profit from the deportation of their countrymen and countrywomen from their own villages. The supposed mutual bond between the lords and their vassals had been broken because many of the vassals had become redundant to the needs of their rulers. The capital-driven financial world that took over had (and has) no humanitarian conscience; profit was (and is) the only consideration. One of the results of this new profit motive was the slave trade, set up to transport African slaves to work on the plantations throughout the British Empire. When the British commons were fenced in the owners had no care whether those who formerly had made their livings from that land were cast down into poverty and starvation. They saw the world in terms of the free market and saw those who were cast out as people who had not enough ability to succeed, who were therefore unworthy of anything better than to live in squalor and hunger. The system had no humanitarian conscience.

There was no such thing as human rights in those days. The establishment approved of and profited from slavery, and the indigenous poor of Britain and Ireland were considered to have no more rights than any other slaves of the empire. Those who could emigrated to industrial towns and cities, where they worked long and dangerous hours in mills and factories with no health and safety regulations to protect them from industrial accidents and illnesses, with no medical care if they were sick or injured, and with the prospect of being imprisoned in the workhouse once they were no longer able to work.

Not everyone was expelled, as some were still needed to work the land. The harsh living conditions, which many country people suffered in Britain before World War I, are something only occasionally touched on in popular fiction: romance novels or television and movie costume dramas. The historical reality of grinding poverty and oppression, which the majority of British peasantry suffered under their lords and masters—both temporal and spiritual—is prettified, with an idealized rural Arcadia presented to the consumer. Nothing could be further from the truth. Fatigue, cold, and hunger were the everyday life of farmworkers. The meager basics of life were scarcely available in the good times, while in the bad times famine was the norm. The suffering was unremitting and lifelong. My ancestress, Elizabeth Hazelwood, living in Ely, Cambridgeshire, in the first half of the nineteenth century, bore thirteen children. Nine died in infancy. It was no rural idyll there for her and her family. The everyday reality of life in that part of England then can be understood from the documented experience of one farm laborer, John Irons of Eynesbury, Huntingdonshire, who lived and worked in the 1860s in an eminently arable and ostensibly prosperous part of rural England.

Breakfast, which was eaten on the farm upon the worker's arrival at six in the morning, consisted of bread brought from home, to which was added milk supplied by the farmer. Lunch was nothing but bread, eaten during a short interval at nine o'clock. Dinner was taken at the farm at two in the afternoon, when the horses had finished their day's work. This consisted of a flour, lard, and onion dumpling and a small piece of fat pork, boiled in a bag and brought from home already cooked. If the farmer's wife was kindly, she might warm up this fare and also give the workers soup. All this consisted of was the water in which meat or vegetables had been boiled. In bad times the piece of pork would be taken home uneaten to give a bit of flavor to the next day's dumpling. Supper was eaten with the family at home, being bread and lard with vegetables. No butter was ever eaten, and bread was made once a week at home and taken to the baker for baking. It was made of grain gleaned from the ground after the harvest.

No wonder a local rural rhyme of the time went:

God made bees.
Bees make honey.
Laborers do the work,
And the farmers get the money.

Medical treatment, if one was taken ill, was fraught with trouble. Doctors charged fees that were far beyond the means of the poor, so people took recourse with the local wisewoman, who was also the midwife who brought babies into the world and sometimes performed abortions and euthanasia (Pennick 2011a, 106–7). There were no paved roads, no piped chlorinated water, no sanitary washing facilities, no electric or gas lighting, no mass communications media, and no machines of any kind except the local wind or water mill and the parish pump.

Enclosure of the land assisted the construction of railways, the private companies that were, of course, financed and owned by the members of the same class who sat in Parliament. Common land that had not yet been enclosed was sought out as a place for the construction of railway workshops, stations, and goods yards; and many roads and trackways were cut by the railway lines, whose companies were given ownership by Act of Parliament. Many routes used by drovers who brought their cattle and sheep into England from Wales and Scotland were blocked by new railway lines. The drovers who remained for the few years before the railway companies took over transport of livestock were compelled to drive their herds along public roads, which they had hitherto avoided when they could. When the railway lines were built, generous areas of additional land were taken by the railway companies and sold to entrepreneurs who built mills and factories that used the railways for transporting in raw materials and transporting out finished goods.

The cycles of the seasons and their associated agricultural festivals all had spiritual and magical elements. Industry, being conducted according to linear rather than cyclic time, abolished the festivals of the year so far as it was possible. Magical techniques, commonplace in rural

Fig. 1.2. Country railway, Welshpool and Llanfair

crafts and trades, were much fewer in the new industries, though until the abolition of horse power, the mysteries of horsemanry were present in industrial environments.

Urbanization increased as towns expanded around railway locomotive, carriage, and wagon works. Established towns like Derby, Doncaster, Swindon, and Crewe became railway towns where locomotives and rolling stock were built and serviced, expanding with new housing and facilities far out into the fields that once surrounded the towns.

Where the new lines were driven through towns and cities, swathes of buildings were demolished, secular and sacred alike. The Midland Railway into London was driven straight through Saint Pancras's burial ground, and the dead were unceremoniously dug up from the consecrated earth and shipped off for mass reburial elsewhere. At the very end of the nineteenth century, also in London, the dead were removed from the crypt of the church of Saint Mary Woolnoth by the City and South London Railway for the construction of an under-

ground station (Horne 1987, 10–11). But new churches also were
built on plots of railway land in the expanded industrial towns for
the workers to attend. In the main these churches were not located
according to geomantic principles, and orientation was often ignored.
Some, clearly located according to Masonic principles, remain today
as notable exceptions to the norm.

By 1900 country remote from towns was crisscrossed by railways.
Railways even crisscrossed nonindustrialized islands like the Isle of

Fig. 1.3. Saint Mary Woolnoth, August 3, 2008
(drawing by Nigel Pennick)

Wight and the Isle of Man. Rural light railways like those at Welshpool and Wissington and roadside tramways like those at Wantage and Wisbech carried farm produce to railheads, where it was transshipped to the main line. Whether this improved the plight of the rural workers is questionable. The rural way of life, after the enclosures, was altered into an urbanized commercial service economy, serving a national market rather than fulfilling local needs. By the middle of the twentieth century the success of motor vehicles after World War I had not only superseded horse traction and abolished the trades of horseman and carter but also had caused the closure of most country railways. The tracks were torn up and in most cases left as abandoned strips of land running across the country. In some places farmers bought the track bed and ploughed it up, reintegrating it into the fields.

But as the railways were being ripped up new transportation and communication links were being made throughout the country. The process of urbanization had been accelerated when the General Post Office extended telephone wires into most parts of the country, and wireless broadcasting brought the London government propaganda of the BBC into every household that had a radio receiver. Before World War II, motoring enthusiasts had admired the motorways constructed in fascist Italy for both their utilitarian aesthetic and the way the authoritarian government could order them to be built wherever they were deemed necessary. National efficiency, it was argued, overruled local interests, and the same thing could be done in Britain. Even in 1928, however, voices were raised against new roads, and Clough Williams-Ellis's book *England and the Octopus* was a major statement against them, arguing for the causes later identified as ecology and conservation against the new arterial roads that, like the tentacles of an octopus, had Britain in their grip.

Although the politics of the corporate state failed to gain much support, the Second World War led to a command economy in which everything was subordinated to the war effort, and afterward it was believed that continuing this way of doing things would "make Britain great again." Airfields and military bases had been built during the war wherever the authorities deemed that they were needed, without regard to the wishes and needs of the locals, who were often expelled from their own villages, never to return. So the same brutal principles were deemed to hold good for peacetime. The countryside was electrified with poles and pylons carrying the cables, and old forms of power went out of use. There was no place for the rural or traditional in this worldview. As special places in the landscape were altered irrevocably or destroyed utterly, their magical, eldritch qualities were obliterated, and the traditional rites and ceremonies performed at them were lost. Even when they remained, in a totally altered context, local knowledge about

Fig. 1.4. The all-metal landscape at Cambridge

them was lost as people moved around to find work or fight in wars, and people's attachment to place was broken.

The time of atomic bombs, televisions, airliners, and rockets had arrived, and the years after the war's end in 1945 were dominated by mostly failed government attempts with the British military-industrial complex to pursue costly aerospace projects like the Bristol Brabazon, the Comet airliner, the V-bombers that carried nuclear weapons, and the rocket called Blue Streak, part of a heroic British space project that was subsequently canceled. The cartoon character Dan Dare was not to be the first man on the moon. Government preoccupation with a forthcoming nuclear war led to the construction in secret of numerous underground bunkers for government, not civilian, use, that were linked by deep-level tunnels (Pennick 1988). These were built under major cities and in unobtrusive country sites where they were intended for government officials and civil servants to flee the cities so they could run the remnants of Britain after the devastation of a Soviet nuclear attack (Laurie 1972). Linking them from 1955 onward, a series of microwave telecommunications towers codenamed Backbone appeared on strategic high points in the landscape (223; 1979, 227–44). They were linked to the government bunkers, the BBC broadcasting facilities, and the nuclear early-warning stations that also visibly altered the landscape of eastern England. Backbone was intended to keep the politicians, civil servants, and military personnel, who would be hidden deep underground in bunkers across the country, in touch with one another after Britain's cities and most of the civilian population had been incinerated by hydrogen bombs.

Part of this military-industrial complex drive was a project for a national motorway system, most of which was actually built. Apart from the need for better roads to cope with increasing traffic, there was, of course, also a strategic post-nuclear-holocaust dimension to some of the earlier motorways' routes. The dispersal of some populations into the new towns that were built at this time also came from this covert preparation for nuclear war. The acquisition of the land on which these

Fig. 1.5. Aboveground section of underground bunker,
Clapham, London

new motorways were built carried on the legal structures set up for the railways. They were compulsorily purchased from the landowners at the market price of the land. The growth of car ownership led to the construction of petrol stations everywhere, in villages as much as in towns and cities, with deliveries of fuel from the refineries. These brought the brash urban corporate design of the oil companies into the most traditional and picturesque places.

Country roads and tracks were progressively covered with tarmac and widened for motor vehicles until only a few old green lanes remained, themselves rutted with the deep tire tracks of monster tractors. On the major roads, to allow the easier passage of motor vehicles, crossroads were reconstructed as staggered junctions, roundabouts, or overpasses. At these places the old magic of the crossroads was obliterated. By the 1960s the old ancestral countryside had been all but destroyed. What still survives exists only as glimpses of a shattered past. During the same period that the motorways were being driven across the land, mechanization of farming was completed, and in lowland Britain large swathes of the characteristic hedgerows, many of which dated from medieval times, were rooted up to make fields larger and easier to work with agricultural machinery, which, in turn, became progressively larger. The process continues.

Invisibly, the environment has been irrevocably altered since the eighteenth century. The noxious emissions of smoke from foundries and factories were noted by writers and singers and seen as a sign of impending doom by the Romantics in the latter part of the nineteenth century. As well as pollution from myriad sources, the world in which we live is filled with artificial radiation. It began with the

Fig. 1.6. Motorway junction in north London

electric fields from electric telegraphs and power transmission. To this radiation was added radio waves from transmitters and later aviation radar. World War II brought microwave telecommunications and radiation from the fallout of atomic bombs. Subsequently, further atmospheric detonations of atomic and nuclear weapons have added to the radiation pollution. Nuclear power stations have leaked, and there have been disastrous fires and meltdowns at the Calder Hall/Windscale nuclear power plant (now called Sellafield). They changed the name there to accelerate collective amnesia about the nuclear accidents. Leaks at Three Mile Island, Chernobyl, and Fukushima subsequently added to the ecological burden of artificial radiation. Mobile phones add to the electro-smog that surrounds us, unseen, but, we can be sure, not without affecting us adversely. Of course, we are frequently reassured that it is all utterly harmless.

Glimpses of a destroyed past have survived into the present day, partly because they exist at places where people want to go. The ubiquity of cars and good roads means that almost anyone can go anywhere. Tourism as a mass pastime dates from the heyday of the railways, when special trains were laid on to carry people to see special events like prizefights, horse races, exhibitions, and royal jubilees, and later to visit picturesque places for a day out. Since the early days of tourism certain places have become famous and much visited. As well as mountains and waterfalls, ruined abbeys and megalithic structures in picturesque landscapes were and are popular. In certain places railways or tramways were built to take tourists to a place of natural beauty, such as the Vale of Rheidol Railway to Devil's Bridge in western Wales, the Snowdon Mountain Railway to the summit of the highest mountain in Wales, and the Giant's Causeway Tramway in the north of Ireland. While steam trains up a mountainside appear quaint and picturesque today, it is arguable that a new line up a mountain would not be tolerated today. The intrusion today is less overt; the modern equivalent is the car and bus parking lot, road signs, lighting, barbed wire, kiosks, and subway at Stonehenge.

Fig. 1.7. Cable car on the Great Orme, Wales

As with the railway up Snowdon, once revered as a holy mountain, the existence of at least some of these facilities actually destroyed the ambience of the place that the tourists wished to experience. Authentic or not, a nice day out, an attraction to visit, is what most people are looking for. Authentic remains of the former way of life before the urbanization of the countryside are popular because of their comparative rarity and because in some of them we can occasionally experience some continuity of the eldritch. The experience of such places may indeed be authentic, such as punting on the River Cam in Cambridge, where the leisure and tourist industry took over seamlessly from the utilitarian use of the narrow poled boats known as punts for river transport. Thus, Cambridge remains one of the few places where traditional wooden boats are made for everyday use. A traditional craft survives because of the leisure and tourism industry. This is an authentic continuation in the place of its origin. But not all places are like Cambridge, for the leisure and tourism industry has also altered places by the sheer number of visitors and the concomitant services such as parking lots, tourist offices, cafés, souvenir shops, public toilets, and video surveillance. By catering to visitors the people of the place may gain a source of employment and even enjoy a level of prosperity that people in similar but non-picturesque places would not. But in the process the place itself may have lost the very qualities that the visitors seek.

The next stage in this process is the creation of totally new places that mimic authentic places. The most extreme version of this mimicry is in theme parks. The first theme parks were in the United States, derived from permanent funfairs (amusement parks in the United States) like Coney Island, the equivalent of the Pleasure Beach at Blackpool. Tours of the back lots of film studios in Hollywood were a lucrative adjunct to moviemaking, and in the 1950s Walt Disney melded this

Fig. 1.8. Punting in Cambridge at Silver Street Bridge

tourist experience with the funfair when he created Disneyland. The days when the circus would cakewalk into town were over, but employees in imaginary circus costumes could march down the ersatz Main Street several times a day to reenact the appearance of the circus coming to town in former times. A surrogate experience in a simulacrum of a real town became part of the nice day out.

But the theme park town is not a real town. It has no history other than its original construction as a permanent film set, which is deliberately effaced lest it dispel the illusion. The fake town has no autonomous life. There are no residents, no individual property in this town. Everything is owned by the theme park company. The buildings are not real buildings constructed for use but instead are there to create an appearance, just like in the movies. The events enacted with them as a backdrop are finely choreographed performances put on several times a day as a spectacle for the paying customers. The same event is repeated day by day; there is no awareness or recognition of the passage of time. The concept of "keeping up the day" is anathema to such a place of three-dimensional showbiz, for the passage of the year is not conducive to giving every visitor the same experience. Only festivals that have a commercial potential—Valentine's Day, Halloween, Christmas, and New Year's Day—impinge on the theme park. They are good for business. But the days of the other expected events continue on in the same way as the other days of the year. Only the weather is there to distinguish one day from another. The magic of such places of escapism is one of illusion, a theatrical suspension of disbelief engineered by the application of psychology and marketing.

The theme park is the extreme example of a visitor attraction. Built from scratch on formerly productive farmland, it is a totally urban experience completely divorced from the place where it is located. Its frame of reference is toward the theme, whether it is the cartoons and movies of a corporate entertainment conglomerate or a more generic one like the Wild West or outer space. As with the movies, television, or the internet, the place where the media are consumed is not important. It is an inward-looking experience, attention being channeled exclusively into the spectacle with no awareness of the outer surroundings that lie beyond the plasterboard walls. It is essentially an urban-industrial aesthetic that has nothing to do with the natural world, other than it has to conform to the physical laws of nature.

There are numerous ways of seeing and experiencing the world, but of all of them, the theme park is one of the most controlled physical environments one can enter. It leaves no mental space for contemplation, no time to stand still and be present. One is moved on as fast as possible from one attraction to the next until one finds oneself at the exit gate—time to go home. Unfortunately, the financial success of theme parks has made them a recommendation or role model for the management of authentic places. So similar attractions are installed at places where the original visitor attraction was to see natural beauty, an antiquity, or a sacred place. Like the accoutrements of tourism, the unintended consequence of this alteration of use may be the marginalization of the essential qualities that the place possessed, or even their destruction. This is where we are, *now*.

2

THE ENSOULED WORLD

Heathendom is . . . that they worship heathen gods, and the sun or moon, fire or rivers, water-wells or stones, or forest trees of any kind.
THE *DOOMS* OF KING CANUTE, 1020–1023 CE

More than 250 years of industrial production have separated the greater part of life in this country from its roots in the natural world. Most of us spend the majority of our time in the artificial environments of towns and cities, inside vehicles, or seeing highly selected parts of the world through the medium of the electronic screen. Because of this almost total separation from the natural world, relatively few people have the opportunity to come into contact with the preindustrial culture of their ancestors. The rejection of the natural world and of the human methods of harmonization with nature is the fundamental basis of the predominant culture of our era.

Of course, even when the natural world is ignored, we are all dependent on it. Our ancestors were more immediately dependent on it than we are, as our contemporary society has massive backup resources that can mitigate famines and natural disasters that would have wiped out our forebears. The beliefs, traditions, and customs of our ancestors survive in contemporary society as mythic fragments that are appro-priated frequently by politics and commerce as signifiers of authentic-ity. Emblems from the past, transformed in the service of present-day businesses and institutions, are often the only signifiers that other ways of thought, feeling, and being existed among our ancestors. It is against this background that we approach the matter of geomancy.

Religions deal with theories of the place of humans in the cosmos. The predominant patriarchal religions of the contemporary West—Judaism, Christianity, and Islam—are grounded in the creationist mythos that God placed man on Earth to subdue it, that the Earth was created as a place in which the human race would be predominant, with the plants and animals put here as resources to sustain us. This belief has informed post-religious materialist doctrine too. Both capitalist industrialists and those who followed Engels's and Lenin's descriptions of nature behave as though the Earth is the property of humans to do with it as they will, to exploit and despoil it without regard to the eco-logical consequences, for the patriarchal religions see humans as above and outside of nature—a dangerous, arrogant, and erroneous assump-tion, for there can be no long-term survival of those things that ignore and flout the workings of nature. We live in a culture in which domi-nance is considered the only criterion of success. Contemporary life is characterized by one-sidedness and extremism, in business, politics, and religion. However, by definition, extremes are unbalanced. If we have total reliance on materialism, we will feel that something is missing, and if we reject everything material for the spiritual, we will suffer a lack in other ways.

During the ninth and tenth centuries of our present calendar, Iceland was colonized by settlers from Norway and the Western Isles of Scotland. Their spiritual response to the landscape is recorded in the *Landnámabók,* the book of the settlement of Iceland (literally "land taking"). It is a unique record, for all other colonizations in recorded history were of lands already inhabited by indigenous peoples, whereas Iceland was uninhabited territory. Also, these settlers were mostly not

Fig. 2.1. Standing stones at Trelleck, Monmouthshire, Wales

Christians, and so they were acutely aware of the spiritual nature of the land. Certain areas of Iceland were not settled at all, being reserved for the *landvættir,* the "land wights." Rites and ceremonies were performed in honor of these landvættir, and offerings were left for them. For example, *Landnámabók* records how Thorvald Holbarki recited a poem in honor of the giant who dwelled in the fire giant Surtur's cavern, and some Icelanders continue to recognize and honor the land wights today.

Folk tradition always taught that there are places where human beings have never been welcome and ought never to trespass. These are not intrinsically bad places, but it is certain that human presence there is inappropriate. It is not very sensible to enter the crater of an active volcano or an enclosure around an electricity substation, so equally to enter such a *locus terribilis* is to court fatal peril. But time and again unknowing, foolhardy, or self-centered people *have* built on a locus terribilis. The inevitable catastrophic consequences of their insolence are recounted in folktale and legend. Dearth and disease, derangement, destruction, and death have fallen on those who dared to dwell on those places where we must not be—not necessarily because the denizens therein have punished the transgressors, but because it is a natural consequence of such an action.

Geomancy is about being in harmony with the place we live, and it is more than just orientation, the management of subtle energies, the placation of spirits, or the placement of individual artifacts. There is a very human tendency to be unaware of what has been done already in the past and so to repeat the same mistakes. Even those who do study history and recognize mistakes often feel immune from the way of the world and act as though *this time* the failings of the past will not happen. There are many sorts of natural places, such as volcanoes, whose physical characteristics are hostile to prolonged human existence there. Subtler than these are spiritually bad places, those whose character, seen traditionally as its indwelling spirit, the genius loci, more often seen in modern terms as harmful energies, is inimical to human presence.

There are geomantic techniques for mitigating the (to humans) harmful effects of these places, and much study has been made of them. Among human-made "bad places" are locations used for the burial of the dead and sites of murders, atrocities, and battles. In all cases the places themselves are not intrinsically bad. It is only human perception that makes them so, because they carry the potential to make human life there difficult or impossible. For other beings, both spiritual and physical, these places may be good. A seaside cliff face is a great place for nesting seabirds but is a difficult place to build a house. But humans often build against their better judgment and try to live in places that are not conducive to human life on a sustainable basis. It is the spectacular failures that pass into history as symbolic instances of this human hubris to live in unsuitable places. The legends of Atlantis and the Tower of Babel are metaphors of overstretched human attempts to go beyond the limits of nature. The more extravagant the attempt, the greater the downfall appears to be.

But the traditional worldview lost out, for the Industrial Revolution overthrew the ancient wisdom and understanding of tradition, and from the industrial worldview came the creed of modernism. In the late nineteenth and early twentieth centuries the German philosopher and economist Max Weber characterized modernism as the progressive secularization, disenchantment, and removal of magic from life. In modernism nature is not spiritual; it exists only for human use. The prophets of modernism preached that nature is not ensouled but rather only dead matter—a resource that man is destined to control and exploit. From the earliest days of industrialization, images of irresistible power and domination were conjured up as the urban invaded the rural. For example, two hundred years ago the entrepreneurs of the East End of Sheffield named their new steelworks after the ancient Greeks' Titans and volcanoes—Atlas, Cyclops, Etna, and Hecla—and Sheffield's Vulcan Road was lined with the fiery furnaces of heavy metal. Nature was obliterated, and night turned to day by the flames, while day was turned to night by the smoke. An eighteenth-century Yorkshire folk song, "The Dalesman's Litany," tells of a countryman from the Dales forced by economics to work in the unnatural and inhumane environment of heavily polluted industrial towns.

I've walked at night down Sheffield Lines
'Twas just like being in Hell
Where furnaces cast out tongues of fire
With a noise like the wind on the Fell.

Sheffield Lines is an example of how industrialization created a new class of place-names. Using the name of the Roman smith-god Vulcan was a knowing tribute that appeared in many places during the Industrial Revolution. On January 30, 1796, the Birmingham industrialist Matthew Boulton opened his new iron foundry at Smethwick with a consecration ceremony: "In the name of Vulcan and the gods and goddesses of fire and water [I] pronounce the name of the Soho Foundry. May that name endure for ever and ever and let all the people say 'Amen.'" In 1837 the first steam locomotive to work the new Great Western Railway was named Vulcan (Burridge 1975, 8).

Traditional names of places and features in the landscape reflected shapes, legends, and people's names. Industrial naming redefined the landscape as industry altered it. Railway tunnels were likened to hellish places, such as Bedlam Tunnel near Radstock, Somerset, and Golgotha Tunnel on the East Kent Railway. Company names became definitive, with places called names like Monsanto Sidings Junction, while industrial processing gave us Teesside's Lockerbie Grids. Royalty gave their names to railway stations, docks, and bridges, such as Victoria Stations in London and Manchester, Queen Alexandra Dock in Cardiff, and both Victoria and Elizabeth Bridges in Cambridge. Conversely, some landscape features were so altered by industry that only the name remained to tell what the place had been before. Dee Marsh Sidings at the estuary of the River Dee in Wales told of a drained marsh laid with railway tracks; Heathrow Airport is no longer Hounslow Heath. The dreary names of so many places actually express very well the reality of them as marginalized dumps at the end of nowhere. Some places have experienced this for more than three hundred years. The traditional way of life, developed over thousands of years, was almost completely ripped apart in a historically short time. In the twenty-first century we are now living in the ruins of both the ensouled landscape and a long-depleted natural environment, with all the deleterious effects that has had on society.

As people living in this given situation, we may pertinently ask what used to be there before modernism, and what comes after it. This is not just the well-debated postmodern dilemma, for it recognizes, as postmodernism often fails to do, premodern magic spirituality and consciousness. Despite the situation experienced by the Dalesman and the prevailing industrial belief that there is no spiritual essence of place, stories from relatively recent times abound of local people warning developers that their new buildings were being put up on land where no building should stand. In the late 1970s, for example, just such a factory was erected at the British taxpayers' expense near Belfast. On the place where the new car factory was to be built grew an ancient and venerable hawthorn tree, ensouled, the locals asserted, by eldritch guardian spirits. Dismissing this as Irish peasant superstition, those who saw big profits in the venture cut it down and bulldozed the land. On this place of ancient veneration arose the notorious car factory of DeLorean. Only three years later it was closed, having made a small number of elite but flawed vehicles and suffering a massive financial loss. Blighted and derelict places where such establishments once existed are instances of the desacralized cosmos.

When humans make things on a human scale according to true principles without the interposition of heavy machinery, then we may produce ensouled artifacts. In the sixteenth century the Italian author and philosopher Guilio Camillo Delminio noted that in ancient Egypt "were sculptors so skilled that when they had given perfect proportions to a statue, it was found to be animated with an angelic spirit: for such perfection could not be without a soul." Like the magician, the spiritual craftsperson enables material to be pervaded with spirit, elevating it above the level of inert substance into a state of ensoulment. Things made by human hands that embody the eternal patterns of the cosmos thereby reconcile transient mundane human existence with the transcendent. As Weber noted, this spiritual understanding of the land we exist on and the materials within it are in stark opposition to the tenets of modernism. Industrial production knows nothing of the spiritualization of matter.

The brutal titanic and volcanic powers after which the Sheffield steelworks were named signify that in this way of life the individual is powerless and will be crushed by overwhelming force if he or she resists. In the nineteenth century the arts and crafts movement, in attempting to continue traditional ways of doing things, promoted a spiritual understanding of the material world. In 1891, William

Fig. 2.2. An Egyptian image of the chief god of the
ancient pantheon, Amun Ra

Richard Lethaby, the doyen of British spiritual architecture, wrote,
"Art is the humanity put into workmanship; the rest is slavery." But
the machine rolled on.

So currently, in the present day, there are two separate and irrecon-
cilable worldviews: a spiritual view of an ensouled world and a materialist view of a world of dead matter, there to be used and used up. Of
course there are positions that oscillate between the two or have elements of both in a disjunctive view of reality. But the traditional view
is unequivocal: the ancient European sages taught that the cosmos is a
single living substance, that mind and matter are one. All things correspond analogously; the largest is reflected in the smallest, as above so
below. In one is all. This holistic unity of being, of space, time, matter,

and life, was expressed by the London mystic William Blake in his poem "Auguries of Innocence."

> *To see a world in a grain of sand*
> *And a heaven in a wild flower—*
> *Hold infinity in the palm of your hand*
> *And eternity in an Hour.*

The traditional view of what it is to be human is totally different from the current ethos of governments and businesses, which pervades even the private areas of individual citizens. Traditionally the individual is not a separate, alienated being but just another economic unit, defined by a number and his or her status level in the economic hierarchy, a part of the great continuum of all things. This is expressed in the traditional relationship of humans to their homeland, where family, life, and place form an indistinguishable unity. Only by trying to recall the traditional understanding of the human relationship with the land can we recover something of the holistic life that once was the experience of everyone and build a different future on it.

3

SPACE AND PLACE

The early-twentieth-century founder of the De Stijl arts and crafts movement in the Netherlands, Gerrit Rietveld, observed that we cannot conceive of existence without space. All physical objects occupy space. Our perception of the world in which we exist as physical bodies is in terms of spatial relationships. Human structures, from pots and boxes to buildings, define space by enclosing and articulating it. When space is handled with understanding, then a tangible reality is created. This is presence. There is no presence without time, and it is within time that all physical things exist. In his seminal 1891 book *Architecture, Mysticism, and Myth,* William Richard Lethaby explained this pattern in a sacred and symbolic context: "The perfect temple should stand at the centre of the world, a microcosm of the universe fabric, its walls built foursquare with the walls of heaven."

Almost three thousand years ago the Etruscans developed a spiritual worldview that related human activities to the landscape and the cosmos. The Etruscans' magical books, the *Libri Tagetici,* otherwise known as *The Ostentarian,* were the repository of the teachings and practices of the Etruscan discipline. This spiritual craft had the means of locating the local *omphalos,* the local "center of the world," and laying out the countryside around it in accordance with the qualities of the

33

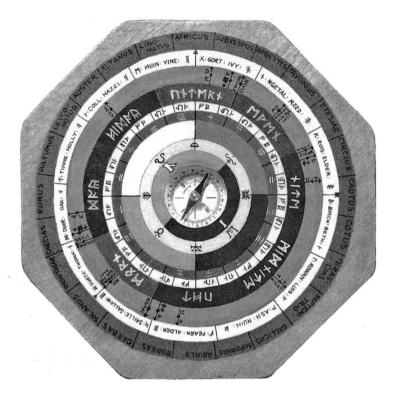

Fig. 3.1. Geomantic compass

directions. To the horizon in each direction, through the omphalos, a straight north–south line, the *cardo,* was drawn. At right angles to this, a straight east–west line, the *decumanus,* was also drawn. This divided the land area into four quarters. Any rectilinear building erected in this tradition, like the perfect temple described by Lethaby, has walls that face these directions. The north and south faces of the walls stand at right angles to the cardo, while the east and west faces stand at right angles to the decumanus; the north and south faces run east–west and the east and west faces run north–south. The building's corners are directed toward the intercardinal points: northeast, southeast, southwest, and northwest. The square plan oriented in this manner produces an eightfold division of space. The Etruscan discipline was used to lay out towns, temples, and the agricultural landscape around a town. It was a system that was adopted by the Romans, and the land surveying system called centuriation, which divided territories into a square grid, was developed from it. When the United States was surveyed, the Roman centuriation grid was used, but the land was measured in English feet.

The geomantic layout of British traditional towns, among them Oxford, Dunstable, Royston, Chichester, and Llanidloes, reflects this cosmological principle. Oxford is significant because the carfax, the meeting of roads, there is said to be the center of Britain in *The Mabinogion,* the collection of the earliest prose stories of English literature, and Cirencester, Dunstable, and Royston are each at the crossing points of two of the four Royal Roads of Britain. Cirencester stands at the intersection of the Fosse Way and the Icknield Way, Dunstable being on Watling Street and the Icknield Way, and Royston on Ermine

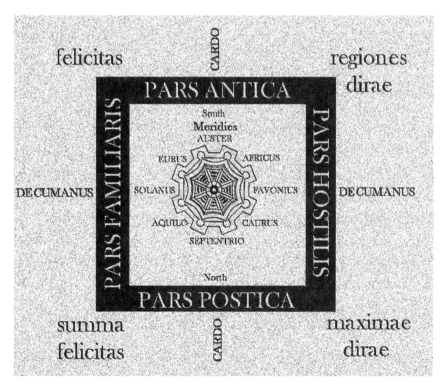

Fig. 3.2 Diagram of the Etruscan discipline and the eight winds

Street and the Icknield Way. The other crossroads on the Royal Roads is at High Cross in Leicestershire, where the Fosse Way and Watling Street intersect. A stone, cross, or church at the central crossroads marks the omphalos. Everything else there, the town and the landscape around it, physically and symbolically relates to this central point.

Based on a square, the sides of the temple or town face the four cardinal directions and the corners mark the four intercardinal ones. In the Northern Hemisphere, when we face southward, to our left is the east, the quarter of the rising sun, morning, and the principle of increase. In front of us is the south, the high point of the sun, mid-day. Right of us is west, the quarter where the sun goes down, evening, and the principle of decline. Behind us is the darkness of night, where the sun is behind and beneath us. Facing south we actually face toward the equator; the North Pole and the North Star are behind us. This is physical reality. Above us are the heavens, below us the earth. The sun, moon, planets, and stars of the sky appear to move clockwise. This is the meaning of being in place, being in the world. For we perceive our bodies to have a fourfold structure: left–right, front–back. Our bodies are bilaterally symmetrical, the left and right sides being more or less mirror images of one another. To each of us, with our awareness centered in our bodies, we can say, "I am at the center of my world. The place where I am at any given time is *the* place, *my* place." The world we experience originates here: wherever we are, this is our center of the world, so wherever we are, we experience being here in a fourfold way. And as each individual is centered on his or her own self, the world can also be viewed as centered at a particular place.

Just as the individual was defined traditionally as a spirit incarnated in a body and that body had a physical location, so the spirit of place was seen as localized at a particular location. This point was usually localized at a crossroads, marketplace, or city, at the center of which was a conceptual or real stone, post, or tree. Symbolically this central point could be projected upward from the Earth's surface into the sky (or starry heavens at night) and downward beneath the Earth's surface into the ground. Traditional cosmologies, stemming from a time when there was no knowledge that planet Earth is spherical, saw the surface of the Earth as standing beneath a sky that rotated, with the sun, moon, and stars bringing night and day. Here in this sky was the abode of the sky gods, who sent down rain, thunder and lightning, snow, and occasional stones. Beneath the surface of the Earth, where things and people were buried, was another world, the Mundus, the underworld. In the Etruscan discipline the Mundus was symbolic of the dwelling place of the Inferiæ, the gods of the underworld. This was seen as the realm of the dead and their divine rulers. Out of this underworld came fire through volcanoes, winds, and occasional wild beasts.

The conceptual line linking these three levels of flat-Earth cosmology is the cosmic axis. It is literalized as the axis on which the sky turns, pivoting (in the Northern Hemisphere) at the Pole Star, around which all the other stars rotate. Below, it extends into the underworld. It can serve as a conduit between these worlds, and the spirit journeys of shamans are along this axis. The painting *The Ascent into the Empyrean* by Hieronymus Bosch (ca. 1450–1516) depicts souls being led to heaven through a tube of light. Bosch's vision is an image that those who have been through a near-death experience would recognize, as is the descent into Annwn, the underworld of Welsh mythology.

In Britain the ancient tradition of this comes via the Welsh bard Llewellyn Sion of Glamorgan (ca. 1560–1616), who collected together ancient manuscripts at Raglan Castle in Wales. These manuscripts were attributed to earlier Welsh bards: Taliesin, Einion the Priest, Dafydd Ddu, Sion Cent, Rhys Goch, Cwtta Cwyfarwydd, Ederyn, and Jonas of Menevia. In this tradition, taken from these early writers, it appears that the cosmic axis links four circles of being, only three being accessible to the human spirit, with the fourth, Ceugant, at the top, the sole abode of the creator Hên Ddihenydd. The underworld is called Annwn; the middleworld, Abred; and the upperworld, Gwynfyd. Moral virtues are ascribed to these three realms. In Annwn, the abyss, "the loveless place" or "the land invisible," evil predominates, though it is not a place of eternal punishment like the Christian hell, for Annwn releases its inmates after a period of repurification, to be reincarnated in Abred. Abred, otherwise called Adfant, "the place with the turned-up rim," is a state where good and evil are balanced, where reincarnated souls live a series of lives with spiritual progression or regression depending on their actions under free will. Gwynfyd is "the abode of the enlightened," a state where gods and human souls who have transcended the cycle of their earthly lives reside. Northern European mythology recounts the travels of heroes and gods up and down the cosmic axis. Welsh literature includes descents into Annwn, and Norse mythology tells of the god Hermod's ride down to Hel in an attempt to rescue Balder from his fate. The Northern Tradition's equivalents of these three stages in ancient British tradition are Utgard or Hel, the underworld; Midgard, Middle Earth; and Asgard, the abode of the gods.

Teamhair na Riogh (Tara of the Kings) was in ancient times the royal capital of Ireland, the most sacred and sovereign place of that island. It was a physical example in the landscape of the fourfold. Geomantically, Tara is one of the few European spiritual and royal centers that remains in existence without centuries of overlay. It is a very ancient central place, the center of the Plain of Fál, itself the geomantic center of the island of Ireland. Tara is an impressive place to see, with great earthworks that remain from the active days of its use. The Mound of the Hostages on the Hill of Tara dates from the Neolithic era, so it has been there at least six thousand years. The complex of spiritual and regal structures that remains includes the Lia Fáil, the Stone of Destiny, a local geomantic omphalos at which the high kings of Ireland were inaugurated. Each year at the day of Samhain, representatives of the four provinces of Ireland—Leinster, Munster, Connacht, and Ulster— gathered there for the Assembly of Tara.

Tara stands at the conceptual center of the fourfold island of Ireland. The halls of the four great provinces stood in their relative positions around the royal hall. The entourage of Munster folk occupied a hall to the south of the site; those of Ulster, a hall to the north; Connacht to the west; and Leinster to the east. The high king's central hall was at the center. The Assembly of Tara was thus an image of Ireland as a whole, and whatever was done there affected the whole country. The macrocosm of the island of Ireland magically reflected what happened in the microcosm of Tara.

From Tara ran the five Royal Roads of Ireland: Slige Midluachra, which took the wayfarer to Emain Macha near Armagh in the north; to the northwest, Slige Asal; to the midwest, Slige Mór linked Tara with Uisnech, the navel of Ireland, the omphalos, and the Western Ocean at Galway. To Tipperary in the southwest ran Slige Dála, and to the south was Slige Cualainn, which ran to Bohernabreena, south of Dublin. These were the Royal Roads, which like their counterparts in the island of Great Britain had a spiritual dimension, guaranteeing royal protection of travelers along them. Of course these roads were unlike modern roads that obliterate the subtleties of the landscape in the pursuit of speed. The Royal Roads fitted into the contours of the land and were suited to travels on foot, on horseback, and in ox wagon.

Aristotle taught that we can perceive the timeless within transitory, temporal things. In his cosmology the cycles of the seasons and the eras on Earth reflect the inner workings of the cosmos. Physical objects may decay in time, but their meaning does not disintegrate with them, being part of eternity. In his 1913 book, *Projective Ornament,* the American spiritual architect Claude Bragdon wrote that "the sublime function of true art is to shadow forth the world order through any frail and fragmentary thing a man may make with his hands, so that the great thing can be sensed in the little, the permanent in the transitory." This traditional understanding is not an abstruse theoretical construct concealed in obscure ancient texts and scientific journals but rather a physical reality of life. Geomancy seeks to translate these transcendent realities into physical form at the most appropriate places.

As living beings we are subject to what the artist-philosopher Wassily Kandinsky called in 1911 the "the universal laws of the cosmic world." The cosmos, of which we are part, has recurring patterns of self-similarity, in space, time, and event. From the smallest particle to the largest galaxy, the same basic principles apply. An awareness of this interconnectedness is very ancient, lying at the very foundations of spiritual understanding. It is encapsulated in the venerable maxim ascribed to the ancient Egyptian founder of alchemy, Hermes Trismegistus: the Hermetic maxim. Simply put, it is "as above, so below." The lesser, or smaller, components of existence, the microcosm, recall the structure and pattern of the greater, or larger, components, the macrocosm. The same structural principles exist in both molecules and galaxies. Human beings are part of the nature of the microcosm, and our physical and spiritual natures reflect the entire cosmos, the macrocosm. All things are thus linked in one great chain of being, which is an interconnected sympathetic system, operating at all levels of existence.

THE PLOUGH
AND THE STARS

There's a time and a place for everything.
OLD ENGLISH ADAGE

The Right Place at the Right Time

Geomancy is all about being in the right place at the right time, and the time when the first stone of a building is laid marks the vital moment when it begins to take on physical reality. Memorable rites and ceremonies are performed, and some kind of symbolic deposit is left buried beneath the foundation stone as a token of the act. Since early times the horoscope of the instant of foundation was considered to denote the future success or otherwise of the building. The art of electional astrology seeks to find in advance the most auspicious celestial configuration to lay the first stone of a building. An appropriate inceptional horoscope is drawn up, and the foundation stone is laid at the punctual time, the precise moment indicated by it. To the building this is the instant of birth, equivalent to the natal time in human astrology.

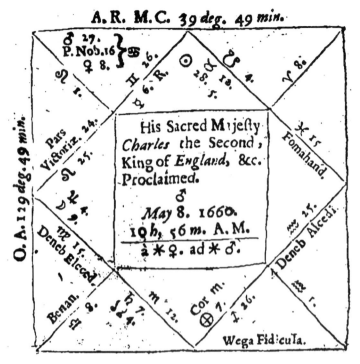

Fig. 4.1. The horoscope of the Restoration King Charles II, 1660

In England at the time of the Restoration of the monarchy, electional astrology was used in the foundation of colleges, institutions, and churches. The foundation stone of the west range of Gonville and Caius College in Cambridge was laid at 4:00 a.m. on May 5, 1565, at the rising of the planet Mercury. In 1675, John Flamsteed, astronomer royal to King Charles II, calculated the inceptional horoscopes for the Royal Exchange, the new Saint Paul's Cathedral (from the seventeenth century), and the Royal Observatory at Greenwich. The Royal Observatory election has the sun in the ninth house, which is appropriate for the philosophical and scientific pursuit of astronomy. The rising sign is Sagittarius, which is the natural ruler of the ninth house, and the beneficent planet Jupiter, Sagittarius's ruler, is in that sign, almost exactly at the position of its rising. By using the inceptional horoscopes, buildings can be placed in a harmonious relationship with the celestial cycles, bringing the users into harmony with the cosmos.

Because Freemasonry was set up as a speculative system in 1717, just at the very beginning of the Industrial Revolution, Masonic ideas and traditions were present as symbolic elements in some industrial contexts. Electional astrology, studied and understood by some Freemasons, clergymen, and gentleman farmers, appears to have played its part in the "turning of the first sod" at the beginning of the construction of factories, canals, docks, and railways. Ceremonial spades engraved with railway coats of arms, dates, and times can be seen in local museums today. They were made for the ritual beginnings of these projects, used once at the punctual time, then preserved as relics. Some of them have outlasted the railway lines they began.

Mills

Machines are far older than the Industrial Revolution, though it was the invention of steam power at that time that made the transformation possible. Before that power had to be supplied by humans, animals, water, and wind. The powered grain-grinding mill is perhaps the oldest machine of all. The traditional mill is an image of the cosmos in which the sky rotates above a fixed Earth as the top millstone turns on the lower one. The old mills in northern Europe were water mills built directly over watercourses (natural or artificial). An axletree with paddles dipped into the water below the mill. The axletree went through a hole in the lower millstone to the upper stone, to which it was connected. Thus, the upper stone turned on the lower stone to grind the grain into flour. Such mills reflected the tripartite cosmos in the Northern Tradition's interpretation: underworldly water (world serpent flowing, Utgard), Earth (fixed lower millstone, Midgard), and starry heavens (upper stone turning, Asgard). And integral to it all, the turning but fixed axletree (Yggdrasil), rotating around a fixed point, the Nail (the Pole Star).

The water mill was a pre- and non-Christian cosmology and technology, for there is no such thing in the Bible. When the Christian religion was imposed on northern Europe, millers were people who operated a technology that was not within the remit of Christian ideology. According to Judeo-Christian dualism, anything that is not authorized biblically is diabolical. But as an indispensable technology,

Fig. 4.2. Windmill, Thaxted Essex

milling continued to operate, and when more complex technology was introduced with gearing connecting to horizontally axled waterwheels, the essential principles of the stones were retained and specialized technological knowledge to operate the first large-scale machinery arrived.

When windmills were invented in Normandy or northern France around 1100, the old water mill cosmology was continued with the stones, though there was now a second cosmological element, the vertical post that supported the mill, arising from crossbeams supporting a trestle that supported the whole structure. A windmill cannot be run backward, because the sails are constructed to operate in one direction. It is often possible to crank the sails the wrong way by using the internal machinery though, if repairs are necessary.

The North Star and the Seven Stars

In the Northern Hemisphere there is a star that stays close to the hub of the night sky as it appears to circle as the night passes. This star has a number of names, its astronomical name being Polaris, the Pole Star. Other names given to it are Tir, the Lode Star, the Nowl or Nail, the Mariner's Star, the Star of the Sea, and the North Star. It can be found in the night sky by following the pointer stars of the constellation of the Seven Stars of the North: Merak and Dubhe. In the United States and Canada this constellation is called the Big Dipper.

The North Star is an important marker in traditional navigation. In the days before radio beacons and then the global positioning system, navigation by the stars was an indispensable skill practiced by all mariners. Travelers on land too, such as the cattle drovers and explorers who had to traverse trackless terrain, also used the North Star to find their way. Symbolically it is the unwavering guiding light that, if we keep our eyes on it, will lead us unfailingly to our destination. Thus it is a symbol of constancy and reliability, the top of the cosmic axis. In religious symbolism the North Star signifies the unfailing nature of God's providence, for it was the Gods' Nail of the Northern Tradition, associated with the rune *tir* before it became Stella Maris, the Star of the Sea, one of the bynames of Our Lady.

The visible arrangement of the Seven Stars of the North has been likened to a plough or a wagon or a big dipper, though astronomically the constellation is called Ursa Major, the Great Bear. Visualized as a wagon, the constellation was called either Woden's Wagon or Charles's Wain (Reuter 1985, 19). Welsh astronomy calls Saith Seren Y Gogledd (the Seven Stars of the North) by a number of different names: Yr Aradr (the Plough), Yr Haeddel Fawr (the Great Plough Handle), Jac a'i Wagen (Jack and His Wagon), Llun Y Llong (the Image of the Ship), and Y Sospan (the Saucepan/Dipper). The Seven Stars themselves are called by their Arabic names: Alioth, Alkaid Benetnash, Dubhe, Megrez, Merak, Mizar, and Phecda. Although, confusingly, the Pleiades sometimes are also called the Seven Stars, Welsh traditional astronomy distinguishes Saith Seren Y Gogledd from Y Saith Seren Siriol, the Seven Cheerful Stars of the Pleiades (also alternatively known as Y Twr Tewdws, the Thick Group).

As with all visible stars, the Seven Stars are ascribed qualities that must be taken into account in astrology. The constellations are, of course, human constructs that enable us to recognize the part of the sky we are looking at. They are named from their imagined resemblance to particular people, animals, and objects. The Greco-Arabic names of the Seven Stars are:

Alioth (or Risalioth), Al Jawn, the Black Horse, with the astrological nature of Saturn and Venus.

Alkaid Benetnash, often just called Benetnash, is also Al Qa'id, the leader of the three draft horses in line that are pulling the plough. According to the astronomer Al Biruni, this brilliant white star was called alternatively Marici, a "ray of light." Astrologically, Alkaid Benetnash is of the astrological nature of the moon and Mercury, and those born at the rising of this star could become tamers of wild beasts.

Dubhe, Al Dubh, the Bear, a yellow star with the astrological nature of Mercury and Venus.

Megrez, Al-Maghriz, the Root of the Tail, a pale yellow star with the astrological nature of Mars.

Merak, Al-maraqq, the Loins, a greenish-white star with the astrological nature of Saturn and Mercury.

Mizar, Al-Misar, the Loincloth, a pale white-emerald double star with the astrological nature of Saturn and Venus.

Phecda, the Thigh, a topaz-yellow star with the astrological nature of Jupiter and Venus.

The Seven Stars is a traditional inn sign in Britain. It is also the sign of freedom. In Saint Thomas Lane in the city of Bristol, the inn called the Seven Stars is famous because the abolitionist campaigner Thomas Clarkson stayed there in 1787 during his investigations into the horrors of the slave trade. Bristol was a major port whose ships were employed in the shameful trafficking, Liverpool and London being the two other major slave-ship ports. Clarkson was hounded by the slavers and just escaped being murdered in Liverpool on the orders of a slave trader. The Irish landlord of the Seven Stars in Bristol refused to be intimidated and braved the violence by permitting Clarkson to stay there. Owing to Clarkson's bravery in collecting data and creating a traveling show of horrific artifacts of the slave trade, an abolitionist movement was started, which finally, through William Wilberforce's parliamentary actions, led first to the abolition of the slave trade in 1807 and finally to the abolition of the institution of slavery itself in the British Empire in 1833.

The Bristol slave-trade businessmen received financial compensation from the government for the loss of their source of income. Many spent it on promoting the Great Western Railway that linked Bristol with London. The first locomotive was named the North Star. Clarkson is commemorated in his hometown of Wisbech in Cambridgeshire by a monument, and a plaque on the outside of the Seven Stars in Bristol commemorates his ethical stand and successful

Fig. 4.3. Seven Stars
(drawing by Nigel Pennick)

campaign against slavery with the motto: "Cry freedom. Cry Seven Stars!"

In the heavens the North Star, Polaris, is pointed to by the stars Merak and Dubhe of the Plough. In the United States this star was called the Freedom Star. In the days of slavery, escaped slaves aimed to get northward to states where slavery did not exist by following the star. The slave-era song "The Drinking Gourd" is a pilot verse in coded language. In African American culture the constellation of the Seven Stars of the North is called the Drinking Gourd, and the song instructs the fugitives to "follow the Drinking Gourd"; that is, to make their way northward.

The pilot verse is an ancient form that was used in sea chanties as a means of preserving and transmitting knowledge of particular passages at sea. The background story about this song tells how it was indeed spread among the slaves by a former seaman, a journeyman carpenter with a wooden leg called Peg Leg Joe, who is the "old man" mentioned in the song's chorus: "Follow the drinking gourd! Follow the drinking gourd. The old man is a-waitin' for to carry you to freedom if you follow the drinking gourd."

The Seven Stars of the North were adopted as an emblem on the flag of the socialist republican Irish Citizen Army, which was founded by James Connolly and Jack White during the turmoil of the general strike in Dublin in 1913. It comprised silver stars superimposed on a plough whose coulter was represented by a sword, all on a green background. Connolly explained the symbolic meaning of "the Plough and the Stars" as a free Ireland that would be in charge of its own destiny from the plough to the stars. The flag was flown by Citizen Army members during the nationalist Easter Rising in Dublin that lasted from the twenty-fourth to the thirtieth of April 1916.

The Plough and the Stars is the title of a play by Irish Citizen Army stalwart Seán O'Casey, first performed in 1926. In the 1930s the flag's background color was changed from green to blue, the image of the plough and sword was removed, and only the stars remained. But, as with many flags that make nuanced statements about politics, the original flag with the plough and the stars appears today in events staged by the Irish Republican Socialist Party, the Workers' Party of Ireland, and Sinn Féin. The very similar flag of Alaska, perhaps derived from its Irish forerunner, was designed by Benny Benson, who was the winner of the flag-designing competition in 1927. The appearance of the Alaskan flag is very close to the Irish republican flag, being composed of eight gold stars (the Seven Stars of the North and the North Star) on a dark-blue background. The Seven Stars are a remarkable instance of human cultural continuity, continuously renewed in novel ways.

5

THE IMPORTANCE OF THE RIGHT DIRECTION

The only fixed solar directions are south, the highest point of the sun in the day, and north, when the sun is at its nadir. All other positions of the sun, rising and setting on the horizon, vary day by day and season by season. Sunrise at the equinoxes is due east–west. The most southerly sunrise is at the winter solstice, after which the sun rises progressively farther north day by day until the summer solstice, when it reaches its most northerly rising point. After this the sun rises progressively southward until the winter solstice comes again. Of course, this is only apparent to those of us standing on the planet as it is a phenomenon of the rotation of the Earth on its axis and around the sun.

The meridional line, due north–south, the cardo of the Etruscan discipline, was of fundamental importance in northern European geomancy too. Settlements were often built up from south to north, the second settler taking the land to the north of the first homestead. The younger son had the rights to the southernmost plot of land (Reuter 1985, 5). On the Moot Hill the king and law speaker stood in the north, facing south, the assembled people facing north. The plaintiff went from south to north to seek official justice, but in legal proceedings that were not considered to be a contest, such as the conclusion of a contract, one part came from the west, the other from the east (Reuter 1985, 5).

Conventional farmhouses in northern Europe in Viking times were oriented east–west so that the owner's high seat on the northern long wall faced the meridian, the high point of the sun in the south at midday. The high seat pillars were carved with sacred images and a representation of God's Nail, the North Star. North was the direction of prayer in the indigenous religions of northern Europe. "Prayer was directed toward the immovable heavenly seat," wrote Otto Sigfrid Reuter. "The northerly orientation of prayer came into conflict with the easterly orientation, the sacred direction of the Church. . . . Germanic prayer was turned toward the pole of the sky, and implied the heavens" (Reuter 1985, 6). Ancient Jewish belief, perpetuated in the books of Job, Jeremiah, and Isaiah in the Bible, claimed that the "sides of the north" were the abode of the devil (Job 26:6–7, Isaiah 14:12–13, Jeremiah 4: 6). Another Jewish tradition tells that humans are born with their face toward the east, so the right- and left-hand directions were, respectively, good and evil; that is, south and north (Taylor, iv, 335).

The biblical separation of the sheep from the goats sends the goats to the left-hand side; that is, the north. Later, in Anglo-Norman heraldry, the right was called *dexter* and the left *sinister,* and these words still have good and bad connotations today. The early Christian apologist Origen (recognizing that the Earth is round) taught that hell was at the center of the Earth and the entrance to it was at the North Pole. Each time the northern lights appeared, this was a sign that the gates of hell had opened, warning sinners of their doom: "The doctrine of fear of the North creeps in everywhere" (Johnson 1912, 335). The Christians took these beliefs to condemn veneration of the north in the indigenous religions of northern Europe.

In her *An ABC of Witchcraft Past and Present,* Doreen Valiente described the church's abhorrence of the north as the direction of the devil, because of its pagan associations (Valiente 1984, 250–51). She notes that the place to look for anything of a pagan nature in an old church is on the north side. "In the east–west churches of the Frisians, who had recently been compulsorily Christianized by Charlemagne, the [Pagan] Danish King Gotrik had northern doors cut out and forced people to crawl through them" (Reuter 1985, 6). In Britain north doors on old churches are often in existence, but many are walled up. In 1899, George S. Tyack wrote, "The north was of old mystically supposed to typify the devil, and a usage prevailed in some places of opening a door on that side of the church at the administration of Holy Baptism, for the exit of the exorcised demon (66). Tyack gave a specific example of this: "In the Cornish church of Wellcombe is a door in the north wall, locally known as 'the devil's door,' which is opened, at the renunciation in the baptismal service, for the exorcised spirit to take his flight" (171).

The meridional line is used in traditional British folk magic. The *diurnall,* or diary, of the conjuring parson William Rudall for January 12, 1665, records how he made a magic circle and set up a rowan staff in a pentacle (also called a pentagram or a pentangle) before standing in the south of the circle, facing due north, to call up the spirit. Another account from Cornwall tells of a toad ritual that involved going from south to north to become a witch or warlock:

> Should any desperate and unhappy man or woman desire to bargain with Satan with a view to gaining the unhallowed powers of witchcraft, the following (so say the Cornishmen) is one way of effecting the purpose. One must present one's self at the altar and receive the Blessed Sacrament; but instead of consuming it, conceal it and carry it away. As the object is blasphemous, we must not be surprised if the means are sacrilegious. Then at midnight this stolen host is to be carried thrice around the church, going from south to north; and at the third time a huge toad will be met, standing open-mouthed. The Sacrament is to be given to this creature, which will then breathe thrice upon the giver, and the latter will at once become a witch or a warlock. (Tyack 1899, 64)

A stream flowing meridionally features in many rites of folk magic. East Anglian toadmanry uses the water of a stream to separate the bones of a toad for magical purposes. In 1915, Catherine Parsons described the toad-bone ritual as practiced in southern Cambridgeshire: "At Horseheath it is believed that, if an ordinary toad be put into a tin pierced with holes and buried in an ant hill until the ants have devoured all the toad's flesh, and the bones be taken out of the tin at twelve o'clock at night and thrown into a running stream, the bones which float up the stream can be used for witching purposes" (37). Another version of the rite was described by the Norfolk horseman Albert Love. He called the ritual the Water of the Moon and specified that it be performed at the full moon (Evans 1971, 217–18). In the region around Cambridge it is considered best that one use a stream flowing north–south for this rite. Ownership of the toad bone gives the toadman control over not only horses but also cattle, pigs, and women, and it gives the toadwoman control over horses, cattle, pigs, and men. The bone bestows on the initiate the ability to see in the dark, to go about "out of the sight of men," and to steal without getting caught. "No door is ever closed to a toadman" is said in the Fens (Pattinson 1953, 425). Toadmen are feared and admired for their extraordinary powers. Of a person who demonstrates these powers and is suspected of toadmanry, it is said that "he must have been to the river."

There is a Welsh tradition that a healing spring should have an outlet toward the south (Johnson 1912, 332). William Henderson records a northern English curing ritual that involved making porridge over a stream running from north to south. The instance recorded by Henderson was performed at a streamlet near a spring head that runs for about fifty yards due south, through a field called Fool, or Foul, Hoggers, near West Belsay. A griddle was placed over this stream, a fire made on the griddle, and porridge cooked on it, and the number of candidates was so great that each patient got but one spoonful as a dose (Henderson 1866, 140). Mention of south-running water is made in a case of witchcraft recorded in a James Raine's *Book of Depositions* from the years 1565 to 1573 (1835). The alleged witch was Jennet Pereson, who was accused of using witchcraft in measuring belts to preserve folks from the fairies and in taking payments to heal people "taken with the fairy." She was said to have sent for south-running water to heal a sick child who they believed had been taken with the fairy and thus fallen ill (Henderson 1866, 140–41). Another instance of healing using south-running water was with the "Black Penny," a talisman belonging to a family stated as "T. of Humebyers." When cattle showed symptoms of mad cow disease, the Black Penny had to be dipped in a well, the water of which ran toward the south, before water was taken from it and given to the affected animals (164).

The location of burials with regard to the direction of the church was significant. Christian burials were made with the body laid west–east, and it was customary to bury the dead in the churchyard to the south side of the church. But bodies were buried on the north side

Fig. 5.1. Graveyard at Bury St. Edmunds

in special circumstances, such as with a convicted murderer. "The sequel to the murder of McDonald by Robert Fitzgerald in Ireland in 1786," wrote Tyack in 1899, citing a contemporary account, was that "the body of Mr. Fitzgerald, immediately after execution was carried to the ruins of Turlagh House. . . . On the next day it was carried to the churchyard of Turlagh, where he was buried on what is generally termed the wrong side of the church, in his clothes without a coffin" (66).

An old Yorkshire funeral custom was that when the cortege reached the churchyard it must on no account go "against the sun," so the procession would sometimes go right around the church to get to the door, rather than take the more direct and usual path. Thomas Pennant says that at Skyvog, in North Wales, the bearers would bring the corpse into the churchyard by no "other way than the south gate" (Tyack 1899, 98). In Lincolnshire it was traditional to reserve the north door for funerals (96). William Andrews notes that in Suffolk, where churches had both a north and a south door, it was the practice to carry the coffin into the church by the south door, rest it at the west end of the aisle, then, after the service, take it out the north door for burial (1890, 137).

6

THE EIGHT WINDS

Greek mythology tells of the winds, when they first came into being, how they were reckless and unpredictable, so the Gods set Aeolus over them as their ruler under the aegis of Juno. This mythos tells that on the Mediterranean island of Lipari, there are caves that are the keeping places of the winds, which can be contained or released at will by Aeolus. Aeolus is the tutelary deity of sails, wind vanes, weathercocks, windmills, washing lines, kites, and the aeolian harp, whose strings produce the modes of the divine harmony. The cardinal points are fundamental, as early classical teachings tell of the four winds that correspond with the four directions: Boreas, Euros, Notos, and Zephyros. Male in character, they are the sons of Astraeus and Eos or Aurora.

The North Wind, called the Sky-Born Boreas by the Greeks and Septentrio by the Romans, was perceived as king of the winds. Boreas is portrayed as a harsh and wrathful force traveling through the upper air, enveloped in mists, driving the thistle heads of autumn across the plain. Nearer the ground Boreas generates whirlwinds of dust and raises waterspouts from the surface of the ocean. The North Wind is personified as a powerful bearded and winged figure, cheeks puffed up with the act of blowing through a conch shell. In Greek mythology his sons, Zetes and Calais—together called the Boreadae—were slain by Herakles and

Fig. 6.1. Tower of the Winds, Athens

transformed into the winds that blow for the nine days that precede the Dog Days. They are portrayed with long blue hair, winged feet, and golden scales on their shoulders.

The East Wind, named variously Apeliotes, Vulturnos, Euros, and Solanus, is personified as an impetuous flying youth, his hair streaming behind him. He broadcasts seeds as he passes across the land, sowing the fertile land to bring forth flowers, fruits, and grain. The South Wind, called Notos and Auster in antiquity and Sirocco today in Italy, is described as the Father of Rain. Notos is personified as a tall man, his hair white with age, dripping wet with rain. In his hands he holds a vessel from which he pours water on those below. His influence is believed to be harmful to human health. The West Wind, called by the Greeks Zephyros and in the Latin tradition Favonius, is depicted as a handsome youth garlanded with flowers, which he scatters across the Earth. He is supported by butterflies' wings and attends Flora, goddess of flowers. The pleasant short-lived breezes called the Zephyrs accompany him, personified as young boys with wings, the images called cherubs in Christian art.

The names of the winds are derived from specific qualities of winds as perceived at Athens and later refined in southern Italy. The developed mainstream European tradition of the winds is received from the Macedonian architect Andronikos of Cyrrhus, who was the architect of the Tower of the Winds at Athens, circa 50 BCE. It still stands. This system recognizes eight basic winds: four cardinal winds—North, East, South, and West and four others located equidistantly between them at the four corners of the heavens. The Athenian Tower of the Winds depicts the eight winds (named sunwise starting at the north): Boreas, Caecias, Apeliotes, Euros, Notos, Lips, Zephyros, and Skiron. They are depicted by carvings that show them in winged human form. The Northeast Wind, Caecias, is depicted throwing down hailstones from the sky; the Southeast Wind, Euros, is an old man clad in a cloak; Lips, the Southwest Wind, steers a ship; while the Northwest Wind, Skiron, throws down fiery ashes from a container. In the Roman tradition described by the architectural writer Marcus Vitruvius Pollio, from which comes the later European understanding of the winds: the Northeast Wind is called Aquilo, the Southeast Wind is Eurus, the Southwest Wind is Africus, and the Northwest Wind is Caurus.

Vitruvius tells us that each of the eight winds has a subsidiary breeze on either side of it, creating a twenty-four-fold division of the horizon. To the west of Septentrio, the North Wind, is Thrascias, and to his east, Gallicus. Aquilo in the northeast has Supernas and Caecias to his north and south; Solanus, the East Wind, is flanked by Carbas on his north and the Ornithiae, which are intermittent breezes, on his south. The Southeast Wind, Eurus, is bracketed by Eurocircias and Volturnus. Auster, the South Wind, has Leuconotus to his east and Altanus to his west. Africus, the Southwest Wind, has Libonotus to his south and Subvesperus to his north. The West Wind, Favonius, has Argestes to his south and the intermittent Etesiae to his north. This wind rose is completed by Caurus, whose flanking breezes are Circius to the south and Corus to the north.

The qualities of the classical winds are not applicable outside the places where they were first recognized, yet they were used to define the compass rose all over Europe, and even by the Spanish surveyors who

Fig. 6.2. Provencal winds

laid out towns in Central and South America. Old maps from Saint Petersburg to Edinburgh, from Milan to Mexico City, and from Lisbon to Stockholm show these eight winds, and in 1992 a tower bearing the Greek wind names was built in Downing College, Cambridge, designed by the classical architect Quinlan Terry. They are a very tenacious example of mythic continuity. But the winds of Cambridge have different qualities, so the winds named in Greek on the Maitland Robinson Library are mere conceit.

Practically, the qualities of any named eight winds are useless outside their proper area. Those who used the wind for their livelihoods, sailors and windmillers, always had their own local names for the local winds, whose characteristics naturally vary from place to place. For example, Nuremberg compasses of the seventeenth century have inscriptions that equate the winds with the weather: north, fair dry; northeast, bright cold; east, warm bright; southeast, fair middling; south, warm humid; southwest, rainy; west, cold humid; northwest, snowy. These are the weathers likely to be brought by the winds in that part of Germany at that time. Like the Greek winds, they differ from winds at other places, and because climate is not a fixed system, but a changing one, they will differ over time too. When they were taken from their original places, the named winds became more a conceptual map of the directions than a system of any practical use. It is as such that they appear in classical magic.

7

BOUNDARIES

Boundaries are primarily about ownership. Property rights, whether private, public, or sacred, define the meaning of areas in culture and in law. Those who claim ownership to areas, which can range from a few square meters to a nation-state, essentially bar access to those areas by those whom the owners consider have no right to be there. This principle applies to areas deemed property as well to as those deemed in the ownership of spiritual beings. Access to space has always been controlled carefully in all civilizations. Concepts of belonging to the group, ritual cleanliness, personal worthiness, and status are necessary for one to have access to an area, whether it be national territory, a private club, or the inner sanctum of a temple. From antiquity religious buildings have been made in forms considered worthy to be the indwelling places of gods and goddesses, and the boundaries around them have been policed to prevent access by those considered profane. In medieval England the holy cities of Beverley in Yorkshire and Bury St. Edmunds in Suffolk had boundaries around them within which various levels of sanctuary existed. This is not an ancient idea whose time has passed: today only Muslims are permitted to enter Mecca; all others are excluded by state law enforced by the religious police. All human boundaries are in some sense imaginary, yet the consequences to the individual of transgressing them can prove catastrophic.

Boundaries are conceptual or physical lines of division between perceived areas, invisible or visible lines of demarcation that separate and define relationships between separated areas in contact with one another. Boundaries can be natural or artificial, passable or impassable. Natural boundaries like rivers, unclimbable ridges, mountains, and seas are obvious to everyone: they create barriers to all who walk; only flying creatures can cross them without problems. Because boundaries themselves are the interfaces between two distinct areas, they are fraught with difficulties. The problems of physical boundaries are self-evident. It is not easy to cross a river without a boat, a bridge over it, or a tunnel beneath it; or a mountain range without going through a pass, which may be blocked by snow in the wintertime. These natural boundaries are geographical givens with which human beings must come to terms. Human-made boundaries, though arbitrary, are invested with the characteristics of natural boundaries, backed up with human force.

Fig. 7.1. Town Wall, Conwy, Wales

Because human-made boundaries are intended to mark the point where the area of "us" becomes the area of "them," potentially they are places of contention and strife. Many fights between neighbors and wars between gangs, tribes, and nations have begun as border disputes. In former times such boundaries were ill defined and ever changing. The history of the border between Scotland and England is so complex that much of its course at different times is unknown—if indeed it was defined at all. For example, the present capital of Scotland, Edinburgh, was founded by the English king of Northumbria, Edwin, as its English name, Edwinsborough, attests, at a time when the border between the English and the Scots (and the Picts) was far north of that settlement. Now it is unthinkable that the present border could be any different.

Human-made boundaries are not fixed forever. They are a process rather than a thing; they are essentially arbitrary and transient. In historical terms they do not last long. The Baneluca around Bury St. Edmunds, a significant spiritual boundary in medieval times, is no longer visible or recognized. In the late twentieth century the Iron Curtain and the Berlin Wall were formidable fortified boundaries between the communist East and the capitalist West, which, it seemed, would last for hundreds of years. They were protected by armed border guards who were under standing orders to shoot anyone who dared to venture into the mine-laden areas that preceded the actual physical barriers. Nevertheless, though many brave or desperate would-be boundary crossers died trying, a few managed to get through. Finally political changes came. The Berlin Wall and the Iron Curtain through Germany were demolished, and although the borderlines once were guarded, forbidden zones of death, one now can walk through them as if they were never there. That is the arbitrary nature of human-made boundaries.

Some human-made boundaries are real even when one could, in theory, cross them without hindrance. In early nineteenth-century London, John Nash designed and built Regent Street as a fashionable

Fig. 7.2. Entrance gateway, Middleburg, the Netherlands

place for the upper classes to shop. But it functioned in a more insidi-ous way, for it served as a barrier between the underclass slums of Saint Giles and Soho and the rich dwellings of the elegant squares of the West End. Regent Street was as much a barrier as any wall dividing commu-nities today. And today some farmers barricade public footpaths, keep a bull in a field to intimidate wayfarers, and plough up the paths, mak-ing them impassable. Like their aristocratic forebears who enclosed the people's common land and took it for their own exclusive use and profit, such farmers unilaterally destroy the common good.

In contemporary times the territories of urban criminal gangs have boundaries unknown and unseen by those who are not involved in gang activities. Non-gang members cross and recross such lines every day without noticing. For a gang member to be found on the wrong side of such a boundary, however, means death. Similarly, cities divided by warring religious sects or ethnicities have boundaries known by all who live there; sometimes even walls are erected along these boundaries to keep the sects apart, as in Belfast. In some cities Orthodox Jewish areas have boundary markers, unnoticed by non-Jews, which allow the devout living inside the boundary to conduct certain activities on the Sabbath, but only inside the boundary. Even when they are visibly of profane origin, delimiting ownership of territory by groups bound together by hatred of other groups, such as gangs, tribes, religious sects, and nations, boundaries have a magical function. They form a conceptual barrier against the "other," a line over which the "other" must not cross upon pain of violent retribution. In this way they are comparable to the magic circles made by magicians and witches, which, theoretically, are created energetic boundaries that enclose and protect the operator while preventing any summoned entities from entering and wreaking havoc.

Magic Circles and Conjuring Parsons

Although they are rarely viewed as such, megalithic circles in the landscape are de facto magic circles, the favored means of the magician who deals with spirits. Whether they were built for that purpose is, of course, unknown and unknowable, but they can certainly serve that function. Fairy rings, patterns on the grass caused by the growth of fungi that are said to be the dancing places of the wild folk, are natural versions of the circles used by human magicians. Chapter 23 of Heinrich Cornelius Agrippa's seminal work of magic, *Three Books of Occult Philosophy,* is titled "Of Geometrical Figures and Bodies, by What Virtue They Are Powerful in Magic, and Which Are Agreeable to Each Element, and the Heaven." Of the circle, the 1651 English edition tells us:

Of these first of all, the circle doth answer to unity; for unity is the centre and circumference of all things . . . a circle is called an infinite line . . . whose beginning and end is in every point, whence also a circular motion is called infinite, not according to time but according to place; hence a circle being the largest [in relative area of any geometric figure] and most perfect of all is judged to be most fit for bindings and conjurations; whence they who adjure evil spirits are wont to environ themselves about with a circle.

The circle functions as the magical protection of the magician who has called up powers that otherwise might destroy him or her.

As Agrippa described it, the demonic empire has customarily been kept from entering the realm of humans through magical boundaries set up by magicians and magician-priests, for historically not only wizards and witches were adept in dealing with spirits. In the West Country, particularly in Cornwall, there was a tradition of conjuring parsons, clergymen who practiced the binding of demons and the "laying" of ghosts. In the West Country, as well as a magical triangular enclosure of ground, a magic circle was known as a "gallitrap," and making such circles to trap and command spirits was the work of the conjuring parson.

The best documentation comes from the seventeenth century, a period when such conjuration by those who were not clergymen laid them open to accusations of witchcraft. So in 1615, at a witch trial in Haddenham, Cambridgeshire, the accused Dorothy Pitman was asked "whether she had at any time made any circle, or did she know of the making of any circle by 'charmer, or enchantment' to do any mischief?" (*Depositions and Informations,* F.10, Ely, 1615, cited in Parsons 1915, 38, 45). A canon authorizing exorcism under the license of a bishop was and is part of the ecclesiastical law of the Anglican Church. An account of the activities of a conjuring parson is recorded in *An Account of an Apparition, Attested by the Rev. William Rudall, Minister at Launceston, in Cornwall,* written in 1665. As noted in chapter 5, Rudall kept a diurnall, in which he wrote of his magical conjuration of spirits. Rudall's book came into the possession of the

Reverend R. S. Hawker of Morwenstow, who published it with anno-
tations (Hawker, 1870, 109ff).

The first case that William Rudall recorded was of a boy, Master
Bligh of Botathen. He had become "morose and silent—nay, even aus-
tere and stern—dwelling apart, always solemn, often in tears." The
cause was ascertained as haunting by the spirit of a certain Dorothy
Dinglet. Rudall went with the boy to the field where he used to meet
the apparition. Rudall himself there saw the ghostly visitor, went back
to the house, and promised the boy and his parents that he would soon
come back and deal with Dorothy Dinglet's ghost.

Rudall noted in his diurnall:

*January 7, 1665. At my own house, I find, by my books, what is
expedient to be done; and then, Apage Sathanas!*

On January 9, Rudall made a secret journey to Exeter to visit the
bishop, and on January 10, he saw the bishop, and having convinced
him, was given official permission to "lay the ghost." When Rudall got
back home, he worked out the astrological chart for the next morning
and prepared his magical paraphernalia.

*January 11, 1665. Therewithal did I hasten home and prepare my
instruments, and cast my figures for the onset of the next day. Took
out my ring of brass and put it on the index finger of my right hand,
with the* Scutum Davidis *traced thereon.*

The next day Rudall rode to the field at Botathen where he had
encountered the spirit.

*January 12, 1665. Rode into the gateway at Botathen, armed at all
points, but not with Saul's armour, and ready. There is danger from
the demons, but so there is in the surrounding air every day. At early
morning then, and alone, for so the usage ordains, I betook me toward*

the field. It was void, and I had thereby due time to prepare. First, I
paced and measured out my circle on the grass. Then did I mark my
pentacle in the very midst, and at the intersection of the five angles I
did set up and fix my crutch of raun [rowan]. Lastly, I took my station
south, at the true line of the meridian, and stood facing due north.
I waited and watched for a long time. At last there was a kind of
trouble in the air, a soft and rippling sound, and all at once the shape
appeared, and came on toward me gradually. I opened my parchment
scroll and read aloud the command. She paused, and seemed to waver
and doubt; stood still; then I rehearsed the sentence again, sounding
out every syllable like a chant. She drew near my ring, but halted at
first outside, on the brink. I sounded again, and now at the third time
I gave the signal in Syriac—the speech which is used, they say, where
such ones dwell and converse in thoughts that glide. She was at last
obedient, and swam into the midst of the circle, and there stood still,
suddenly. I saw, moreover, that she drew back her pointing hand. All
this while I do confess that my knees shook under me, and the drops
of sweat ran down my flesh like rain. But now, although face to face
with the spirit, my heart grew calm, and my mind was composed. I
knew that the pentacle would govern her, and the ring must bind, until
I gave the word. Then I called to mind the rule laid down of old, that
no angel or fiend, no spirit, good or evil, will ever speak until they have
been first spoken to.

The conjuring parson then questioned the spirit under the power of magical compulsion and discovered that the spirit was unquiet because of a certain sin. He demanded what sign the ghost could give that she was a true spirit and not a false fiend, and she predicted that before the next Yuletide, a fearful pestilence would lay waste the land. (This was a prediction of the Great Plague of 1665.) Asked why she so terrified the lad, she replied, "It is the law; we must seek a youth or a maiden of clean life and under age, to receive messages and admonitions."

Rudall allowed the spirit to depart and returned the next day.

January 13, 1665. At sunrise I was again in the field. She came in at once, and, as it seemed, with freedom. Inquired if she knew my thoughts, and what I was going to relate? Answered, "Nay, we only know what we perceive and hear; we cannot see the heart." Then I rehearsed the penitent words of the man she had come up to denounce, and the satisfaction he would perform. Then said she, "peace in our midst." I went through the proper forms of dismissal, and fulfilled all as it was set down and written in my memoranda; and then, with certain fixed rites, I did dismiss that troubled ghost, until she peacefully withdrew, gliding toward the west. Neither did she ever afterward appear, but was allayed until she shall come in her second flesh to the valley of Armageddon on the last day.

Another conjuring parson, Reverend Thomas Flavel, who died in 1682, was commemorated in the church at Mullion in south Cornwall. His memorial read:

> *Earth, take thine Earth, my Sin let Satan havet.*
> *The World my goods; my Soul my God who gavet;*
> *For from these four—Earth, Satan, World, and God—*
> *My flesh, my Sin, my goods, my Soul, I had.*
>   (Rees 1898, 250)

Flavel was the classic conjuring parson; he was credited with the power of laying ghosts, for which he was in great demand. He owned and used books of "the black art," and against the ghosts he used a stick or a whip. A story recounted in 1898 by the Reverend R. Wilkins Rees tells us:

One morning when Flavel was engaged in the service at church, a prying servant entered his sanctum, and incautiously opening a book on the black art, raised at once a legion of evil spirits. Through his power of second-sight the parson became aware of this as he was reading the prayers. He abruptly closed the service, and returned in haste to the vicarage. There he found the poor servant still in the study, distracted with fear and tormented by the spirits. Quickly seizing the book, Flavel proceeded to read backward the passages at which the girl had glanced, all the while striking in every direction with the stout walking-stick that he carried. The spirits were soon dismissed, but not before they had so abused the servant that for days she bore evidences of their violence! These extraordinary powers caused Flavel to be summoned to the aid of many far and near. (250–51)

Like any cunning man, Flavel charged for his activities. A charge of five guineas, an enormous sum, was demanded by him to "settle a ghost that for long had baffled and defied all other skill." Rees recounts how

because of such an expenditure, two men interested in the matter thought that the exorcist should be watched so that they might be satisfied as to the performance of his task. . . . At the appointed hour Flavel arrived, armed with a heavy whip and a book of divination. Crack went the whip, and both the spies started in fear! Each caught sight of the frightened face of the other, and in dread alarm at what seemed a ghostly appearance ran as though for life, leaving the vicar to settle accounts in his own fashion with the spirit. (251–52)

When Flavel died, his own ghost was "laid" by a clergyman, of whom he had said, "When he comes I must go."

As far as can be told from the records, conjuring parsons appear to have practiced a form of folk magic common with other cunning men. Parson Corker of Lamorna was a noted "huntsman, ghost-layer, and devil-driver." As with Rudall, making a pentagram was part of his rites for subduing spirits: "The parson . . . drew the magic pentagram and sacred triangle, within which they placed themselves for safety, and commenced the other ceremonies, only known to the learned, which are required for the effectual subjugation of restless spirits" (Rees 1898, 256).

The Reverend Jago, vicar of Wendron, was another celebrated conjuring parson. "Of Jago it was said that, though he used to ride far and wide over the moorland of his parish, he never took a groom with him, for the moment he alighted from his horse he had but to strike the earth with his whip to summon a demon-groom to take charge of his steed" (Rees 1898, 260). More likely, the parson had the Horseman's Word, the knowledge of how to make a horse stand when bidden. In the eighteenth century Parson Woods of the parish of Ladock was a practicing conjuring parson. He was reputed to be a master of spirits and used as a walking stick a staff made of ebony that had a silver head embellished with a five-sided figure and a silver band bearing the signs of the zodiac and other sigils. "Parson Woods usually dealt with obnoxious spirits in a summary fashion. By some magic rite he made them incarnate in the form of any brute he might fancy, and then gave them an unmerciful horsewhipping" (258).

A mid-eighteenth-century vicar, the Reverend Richard Dodge from Talland in Cornwall, was another conjuring parson.

[His] authority over the spirit world was simply supreme. With him the slightest effort of the will sufficed to raise or "lay" the inhabitants of the other world, and a nod of the head to send any troublesome ghost to that safest of all spirit prisons, the depths of the Red Sea. His people held him in the deepest dread, and all shrank from any nightly encounter with one who, in the hours of darkness, would be preceded, almost invariably, by a host of evil spirits whom, with unsparing hand, he would be driving before him. (Rees 1898, 253)

Conjuring parsons not only cast magic circles and expelled demons but also provided charms and talismans for protection and advantage. The Cornish story of Jackey Trevail and his wrestling match with the devil, recounted by William Bottrell, tells how the conjuring Parson Wood helped him by giving him a charm. He told Trevail, "You must keep your word with the devil. . . . I shall not go with you, yet depend on it I'll be near at hand to protect you against unfair play."

While saying this, Wood took from his pocketbook a slip of parchment on which certain mystic signs and words were traced or written. "Secure this in the left-hand side of your waistcoat," said he, in giving it to Trevail. "Don't change your waistcoat, and be sure to wear it in the encounter; above all, mind ye—show no fear, but behave with him precisely as you would with any ordinary wrestler, and don't spare him, or be fooled by his devices" (Bottrell 1880, 6).

Even if this is just imaginative fiction, the provision of a talisman to win at wrestling is not. The ancient wrestling tradition of Cornwall, like that recorded in Iceland, had its own magical talismans for winning. The Icelandic equivalent was *glímalgaldur,* in which runic talismans were placed in the shoes (Flowers 1989, 100). Knowledge of these runes and other magical spells and sigils was also maintained by the Christian clergy.

The conjuring parsons were numbered among "the astrologers of the west" by the "Old Celt," William Bottrell, who described "the bettermost class of farmers, or rather gentlemen-farmers, as they all resided on, and farmed their own estates," who practiced astrology, which may have been a euphemism for natural and ritual magic. Astrology as an art was not frowned upon so severely as the practice of magic, which was both admired and feared and was extremely suspect to the more religious.

Many of this class were kept long enough at a grammar school, in Penzance, or elsewhere, to learn a little Latin and mathematics; at least they acquired a sufficient knowledge of mensuration to enable them to measure their own fields. Many of those gentlemen were so much given to the study of astrology that they were regarded as conjurors by their domestics and more ignorant neighbours, who, seeing the horoscopes and schemes in the gentlemen's old books, believed these strange-looking figures to be the secret signs of the means used for dealing with the invisible world, or for commanding the spirits of light and darkness, over whom it was devoutly believed that many skillful astrologers of the west had (by means of their books) perfect control. Among the most noted adepts in this science, the best known were Parson Corker, of Buryan; Mr. Jenkyn, of Trezidder or Alverton; Dr. Maddron, of Saint Just; Mr. Ustick, of Morvah; and Mr. Matthew Williams, of Mayon. (Bottrell 1880, 141)

Bottrell told a story about one of them, Matthew Williams of Mayon, which demonstrated his power of binding.

It was found that the gentleman's furze rick was diminishing much faster than could be accounted for, for the consumption of fuel in his own house. He consulted his books, and discovered by his art that some women from the Cove made a practice of carrying away the furze every night. The very next night, after all honest folks should be in their beds, an old woman of the Cove came as usual to the rick for a burn of furze. She made one of no more than the usual size, which she tried to lift on out half the furze, but was still unable to lift the faggot or so left in the rope. Becoming frightened, she tried to get out the rope and run, but found that she had neither the power to draw out the rope, nor move from the spot herself. Of course, the conjuror had put a spell on her, and there she had to remain throughout the cold winter's night, until Mr. Williams came out and released her in the morning from the spell, and as she was a very poor old soul let her have a burn of furze, but she took good care never to come any more, nor any of the rest of the women, who soon found out how she had been served (141).

These puerile stories, and many more of the same class, often recounted about Mr. Williams, and many other gentlemen comparatively well educated for those times, are not without some significance, as they denote the power that in all times and places may be acquired by the learned over the minds of the ignorant, through their fears of the mystical and unknown. (Bottrell 1880, 142)

Rees tells that, as a rule, a conjuring parson was supposed to conduct the ghost-laying ceremony

in Latin, a language that struck the most audacious spirit in all the world with terror. The penalties imposed by the ghost-layer were various. The ghost of Mrs. Baines, which haunted Chapel Street, Penzance, was bound by a powerful exorcist, Parson Singleton, to spin ropes of sand from the banks on the western green for a term of a thousand years, unless she, before that time, spun a rope sufficiently long and strong to reach from Saint Michael's Mount to Saint Clement's Isle. Some knowing ones have asserted that generally these obstreperous ghosts might be laid for any term less than a hundred years, and in any place or body, full or empty, which was very convenient; as, for instance, a solid oak, or the pommel of a sword, or a barrel of beer, if a farmer or simple gentleman, or a butt of wine, if a county magistrate, a big squire, or a lord. But of all places . . . that which a ghost least liked was the Red Sea; it being related that ghosts have prayed their exorcists not to continue them in that place. It was nevertheless considered an incontestable fact that there was an infinite number laid there, perhaps from its being, somehow, a safer prison than any other nearer at hand; though neither history nor tradition gives us any instance of ghosts escaping or returning from this kind of transportation before their time. (1898, 266–67)

The banishment of spirits to the Red Sea by conjuring parsons of the West Country reflects the northern European traditional recognition of a kingdom of the dead beneath large bodies of water, both lakes and the open sea. The English word *soul* comes from an early Germanic word meaning "belonging to the lake," referring directly to this ancient belief (Hasenfratz 2011, 72). In the Northern Tradition seabound souls went to the goddess Ran, and in much later nautical tradition to Davy Jones, in whose locker they are housed. Those who die on land may also go into the waters, to be reborn later as new babies. The motif of a baby being delivered by a stork is a remnant of this belief.

8

CHURCHYARDS AND GRAVEYARDS

They tell me the graveyard . . . is a low-down dirty place.
JOHN LEE HOOKER, "GRAVEYARD BLUES"

The graveyard is a special type of magical enclosure. In many cases the layout of the city of the dead reflects that of the city of the living, but the function of the graveyard is a place to keep the ghosts or spirits in. In mainland Europe the Capitularies of Charlemagne (789 CE) ordered that all Christians must be buried in cemeteries and that traditional burial in barrows (burial mounds) was pagan and forbidden. The distinction arose between a "Christian burial" in consecrated ground and burials elsewhere. Many of the ancient Welsh accounts of early sainted missionaries contain descriptions of divination, *ostenta* (signs), and geomantic actions showing a concurrence between pagan and Christian practice at that time. The accounts of the making of Celtic Christian graveyards have some of the elements of much later British graveyard folklore. *The Life of Saint Cadoc* recounts that, around the year 518 CE, Cadoc founded a monastery at Llancarfan. He made a large earthen mound to be the cemetery "in which the bodies of the faithful might be buried around the temple." In 563 CE on the holy island of Iona, Saint Columba founded a monastery with a laid-out graveyard. One of Columba's followers, Odhran, volunteered to be buried alive in the new cemetery as the first interment. They buried him, and his ghost became the graveyard's supernatural custodian, known ever since as Reilig Odhran.

Tyack wrote 1,336 years later:

There is a superstition in many places that it is something worse than unlucky to be the first corpse buried in a new churchyard; the Devil, in fact, is supposed to have an unquestionable claim to the possession of such a body. In Germany and in Scandinavia the enemy is sometimes outwitted by the interment of a pig or a dog, before any Christian burial takes place. For a long time the people were unwilling to use the churchyard of Saint John's, Bovey-Tracey, for this reason; and only began to do so after a stranger had been laid to rest therein. The same idea prevails in the North of England and in Scotland. There can be little doubt that in this we have a relic of the Pagan custom . . . namely, the offering of an animal, or even of a human, sacrifice at the foundation of a new building. (1899, 80)

It seems that the extreme assisted suicide of Odhran was no longer considered a good idea and that it was undesirable to bury even the body of one who had died naturally in a new graveyard.

According to one tradition it was the rule at one time to provide each church and churchyard with a ghostly defender against the spells of witches or their diabolic practices. In order to do this a dog or a boar was buried alive under one of the cornerstones of the building, and its apparition kept off all profane intruders. In case any person buried in the churchyard is unable to rest but haunts the place at night, the ghost may be laid (so at any rate it was supposed in Staffordshire not very long ago) by cutting a turf, at least four inches square, from his grave, and laying it under the altar for four days. (Tyack 1899, 59)

By the twentieth century the fear of being the first to be buried in a new graveyard seems to have diminished. But even if one is not taken by the devil or one's shade is forced to guard the boundaries against intrusion, the actual location of the first grave in a new cemetery was still considered significant by some who observed tradition. At Bloxwich in the Black Country in 1943 took place the funeral of Patrick Collins, "the King of the Showmen." The ritual selection of the site of his grave by his son was reported in the *Sunday Express* for December 12, 1943.

There was a strange incident at the cemetery when the old man's son visited it accompanied by Father Hanrahan, of Saint Peter's Catholic Church, Bloxwich, to select a site for the grave. When he came to seek a site for his father's last resting place it was found that the Catholic portion of the cemetery was full. The adjoining land, which belongs to the cemetery, was specially consecrated. When Mr. Collins went to select a place for the first grave, he brought his foot forward, raised it and brought his heel down sharply on the turf, making a deep dent in it, exclaiming as he did so, "This is the spot. I want the exact centre of my father's grave to be over that mark." He explained to the priest: "My father used those words and that gesture for 60 years every time he inspected a fairground site to indicate where the principal attraction, usually the biggest of the merry-go-rounds, was to be erected. He never measured the ground, but the chosen spot was always in the exact centre of the showground. It was a ritual with him."

Collins was duly buried at the center of the new graveyard, the first interment. The center point is the place of foundation, as in the

Etruscan Discipline. It is fitting that a king, if only the "King of the Showmen," should be buried in the middle. Those buried after him became, in effect, his entourage.

Because for a very long time most burials in the British Isles were under the aegis of the Christian church, oriented graves were the norm. The explanation for this was usually ascribed to the doctrine of resurrection of the body at the Last Judgment, as explained by the Venerable Bede: the "Sun of Righteousness" would come from the east, and the dead should therefore face the sunrise (Johnson 1912, 244). In Wales, a byname for the east wind was "the wind of the dead men's feet" (Howlett, in Andrews 1899, 136). This orientation was adhered to for the greater part of Christian practice, but once the church split into sectarian factions, Protestants began to defy the necessity for orientation. Puritans, going against everything they saw as "Pope-ish," were among the first to request that they should not be buried in the Catholic direction. In 1589, Martin Month (only famed for this instruction) was duly buried north–south, and subsequent dissenters gave instructions to be buried the same way (Johnson 1912, 244–45).

A Scandinavian folktale tells how, once upon a time, some gravediggers buried a man called Jón Flak in a north–south grave. Every night after he was buried, Flak's ghost appeared to the gravediggers and said to them:

> *Cold's the mould at choir-back,*
> *Cowers beneath it Jón Flak,*
> *Other men lie East and West,*
> *Every one but Jón Flak*
> *Every one but Jón Flak.*

The haunting went on until the gravediggers exhumed Flak and buried him in the proper orientation, after which his ghost was seen no more (Craigie 1896, 301). It appears from this story that proper orientation was considered necessary to prevent the corpse from walking, equally as much as it was deemed necessary for the corpse to be laid in a churchyard and thereby "integrated into the Communion of the Saints" (Hasenfratz 2011, 70).

Ironically, bones of exhumed saints have been revered as holy relics since the early days of the Christian church, when it was necessary to have relics to conduct properly the foundation rites of a new church. At places where famous relics were housed, special shrines were built to exhibit the bones to pilgrims, and the remains of Saint Cuthbert were carried around Northumbria in a ritual perambulation lasting several years (Pennick 2010b, 85–88). The bones of saints were used to empower everything from the weapons used by warriors on the battlefield to healing water used as a remedy for the sick; the rituals are indistinguishable from magic.

Earth, dust, and bones taken from graveyards appear as *materia magica* in many recipes from traditional European witchcraft, Obeah, and hoodoo. Tyack, writing in 1899, noted, "The consecrated soil of a churchyard is a protection against the power of spells, and in Wales people have been known to gather some of it and scatter it upon themselves and their possessions to prevent them from being 'overlooked'" (64–65). Being overlooked is suffering the effects of the evil eye. Graveyards are the initiation places of bonesmen, members of a secret society who are said to carry human knucklebones with them, ostensibly to prevent cramps. The Northamptonshire folklorist Thomas Sternberg noted someone carrying a human kneecap for the same reason (1851, 24–25). An East Anglian tradition tells how a person will see visions if one drinks ale containing the ashes of human bones. Ghosts can be summoned by playing a whistle or flute fashioned from a human bone. So although it has always been illegal to take human bones out of graveyards, traditional magic has many uses for them.

Paradoxically, the consecrated Christian churchyard was also deemed to be a good place to meet the devil. A Cornish churchyard toad-as-devil rite has already been described in chapter 5. From northeastern England came another church/devil ritual: "He, for instance, who 'maketh haste to be rich,'" wrote George S. Tyack, "may gain a large sum of money if he can tie up a black cat with ninety-nine knots, and, taking it to the church door, succeed in selling it there to the Devil under the pretence that it is a hare. Such is a Northumbrian belief, but one wonders if even a man from 'canny Newcastle' could so easily deceive the Prince of Darkness" (1899, 64).

Monuments in graveyards record the names of those who lie there. The titles, medals, and deeds of the dead may also be recorded. But it is traditional to do more than that, for an epitaph is a means for the dead to admonish the living. The voices of the dead appear to speak to us in traditional epitaphs, such as:

> *Remember, as you pass me by,*
> *As you are now, so once was I.*
> *As I am now, so you must be.*
> *Prepare thyself to follow me.*

Of course, not all graveyard epitaphs are as uplifting . . .

> *Watch and pray: for ye know not when the time is.*
> *We should all write our own epitaphs, before it is too late:*
> *He rambled 'til the Butcher cut him down.*

9
STANDING AT THE CROSSROADS

In the traditional landscape there were many more crossroads than there are now. In the days before motor vehicles, the slowness of road transport, even on horseback, meant that collisions at places where roads crossed were minimal. Once motorization took place, precautions were necessary to prevent collisions, and main roads were modified with dogs' legs, staggered junctions, roundabouts, and overpasses, and many traditional crossroads were destroyed. This present reality does not, of course, alter the symbolism and magic of crossroads. Through the archetypal crossroads, at right angles to the ground, runs a conceptual line, the cosmic axis. This leads below to the underworld and above to the upperworld. The crossroads, especially when the roads are oriented toward the four cardinal directions, is thereby a central place that links the four corners of the world with other spiritual dimensions, a place where one may access the domains of gods, spirits, and the dead.

In the days of public executions, people were often hanged at crossroads. Those executed at crossroads gallows and not left to hang as a warning to others were buried close by, often under the road itself, "out of the sanctuary"; that is, not in consecrated ground (Glyde 1872, 28–29). It was formerly British practice to bury suicides at midnight, with a stake driven through their bodies, at crossroads. The law of England actually stipulated that the suicide should be buried in the King's Highway (Halliday 2010, 82). These traditions reflect the old Germanic belief that a dead person could continue to exist in the grave and come out of it as a revenant, a "living corpse" (Ström 1975, 181–94). People possessing "second sight" were believed to be able to see the dead in their graves and hear their singing. The living corpse appeared like a normal person, except its powers greatly exceeded those of a living person, making it extremely dangerous (Hasenfratz 2011, 71). To preempt this possibility, especially if the person had been a criminal in life or had suffered an untimely death and was therefore unlikely to rest in peace, a stake was driven through the body; it was bound magically with woolen threads or covered with wicker basketwork (Tacitus 1959, 28–29) or thorn bushes (Hasenfratz 2011, 70) and weighted down with heavy stones, as recorded in *Grettis Saga*. This ancient tradition has now become entangled with later vampire lore.

A thirteenth-century account in *Eiriks Saga Rauða,* the record of the Norse colony in Greenland, tells how people who died at times when the weather made it impossible to take their corpses to churchyards were buried provisionally in the unconsecrated ground at their farms. A stake was driven through the body and heavy stones were piled on the grave. When the weather was better, a priest arrived, the stake was pulled out, and holy water was poured into the hole made by the stake. The body was then taken to the nearest church and given a Christian burial. Until the nineteenth century the British custom of burial in the road stipulated that heavy stones be placed over the body in a similar way, and suicides were staked just as in the days of northern heathenism.

Bob Trubshaw has observed that in southern England, many pagan burials from the Anglo-Saxon period are found near parish boundaries, which may postdate the burials (1995, 4–5). William Harrison, in 1577, wrote, "Such as kill themselves are buried in a field with a stake driven though their bodies" (Harrison 1968, 190), and John Weever, writing in 1631, noted, "We used to bury such as lay violent hands upon themselves in or near to the highways, with a stake thrust through their bodies, to terrify all passengers that by so infamous and reproachful a burial; not to make such their final passage out of this present world" (22).

The souls of people who committed suicide were thought not to leave the Earth but to become Earth-bound spirits, extremely dangerous to living people (Tebbutt 1984, 17). In former times crossroads were places to avoid at night, if at all possible, especially on certain dates when the returning dead were most likely to be abroad. In the middle of the nineteenth century, Thomas Sternberg recorded how in Northamptonshire on Christmas Eve, "Rustics, also, carefully avoid crossroads on this eventful night, as the ghosts of unfortunate people buried there have particular license to wander about and wreak their evil designs upon defenceless humanity" (1851, 186). More generally, Marie Trevelyan noted a belief that in Wales the dead appear at crossroads at Halloween (1909, 254).

There are many documented cases of burial beside or under the road, mostly of suicides or suspected ones. *The Chronicle of Butley Priory* (in Suffolk) records that in 1509, the prior, Robert Brommer, hanged himself after he financially mismanaged the accounts. He was buried in the parish church, but in September 1510, his body was dug up "and buried again by lay hands outside the sanctuary, that is in the nearest road leading from the said church as far as the way called Hausen Street" (Dickens 1951, 25–26). The parish register of Palgrave in Suffolk notes in the year 1587, "Johannes Bungay sepultus in via" (John Bungay buried in the road), and at Nayland in the year 1599, "29 November was buried at Horsecroft's Gate Robert Myles who did hang himself" (*East Anglian Miscellany* 1940, 32; 1943, 10).

In his 1890 book *Curiosities of the Church: Studies of Curious Customs, Services, and Records,* William Andrews notes an entry in the parish register of West Hallam. Under the date of April 13, 1698, it states, "Katherine the wife of Tho. Smith alias Cutler was found felo de se by ye Coroners inquest & interred in ye crosse ways near ye wind mill on ye same day" (*felo de se* is "suicide"). Andrews also notes that in the "Local Notes and Queries" of the *Nottinghamshire Guardian* for October 29, 1887, "appeared a curious note on this subject. About one and a half miles south of Boston, on what was called the low road to Freiston, a very ancient hawthorn tree marked the spot, and the tree itself was said to have sprung from the stake which was driven through the body of the self-murderer." Thorn bushes were used as one of the binding materials in ancient Germanic burial magic. The Lush Bush at Harleston in Norfolk was reputed to have been a tree that grew from the stake rammed through the body of Mary Turrel in 1813. Accused of drowning her newborn baby girl, Turrel poisoned herself. So she was "buried in the highroad with a stake driven through her body" at the Lush Bush (*Bury and Norwich Post,* 7, April 21, 1813).

Ceremonial disposals at crossroads took place in the case of two hangings of horsekeepers in Cambridgeshire in the eighteenth century. At Oakington in 1768, Richard Cole, a horsekeeper, was found hanging and was buried "in a crossway with a stake drove through his body" (*Cambridge Chronicle,* June 18, 1768), and at Fen Drayton in 1775, John Ashby, another horsekeeper, who "hanged himself," was buried in the highway (*Cambridge Chronicle,* March 18, 1775). Perhaps these hanged men were not suicides at all but rather breakers of the Horseman's Oath, by which they swore not to reveal secrets of their guild, and they were executed for this by their comrades. There was scarcely any meaningful investigation of the cause of deaths before the formation of police forces in the nineteenth century. Forensic investigation was rudimentary or absent, and the "obvious" cause of death was good enough for the authorities. Case closed.

The famed wisewoman Daddy Witch of Horseheath, Cambridgeshire, was said to have been buried in the road. In Cornwall a crossroads about a quarter of a mile from Wendron Church is where the conjuring parson Jago laid the ghost of a poor suicide who had been buried there. "It was supposed that no spirit walking the earth could resist the spells of this mighty parson," Rees tells us, "and that he could even make ghosts appear as marks of delicate attention to those who might be walking with him" (1898, 26). Burial of outsiders, suicides, highwaymen, witches, and Gypsies under the road or next to it was finally deemed to be no longer desirable. By the early nineteenth century new road-making techniques, developed for the turnpikes, were being applied widely, and the authorities did not want to disrupt new, better road surfaces by digging them up needlessly for burials. In 1823 the Royal Assent was given to an act "to alter and amend the law relating to the interment of the remains of any person found *Felo de se*." It directed that the bodies of suicides be buried without a stake being driven through their bodies and that the interments be in the churchyard or other burial ground, and be made "within twenty-four hours after the Coroner's inquest, and between the hours of nine and twelve at night" (Andrews 1890, 165–66).

The crossroads is a place of magical action in vernacular magic from Central Europe, Scandinavia, the British Isles, the United States, and West Africa. It features largely in the American hoodoo tradition, where the actions of disposal and conjuration are versions of the same principles in Europe. The crossroads provides a place where diseases can be shed and transferred to the next person who passes by, where magical items can be made or empowered, and where the otherworldly denizens can be petitioned for assistance. Stories of a musician taking his guitar to a crossroads at night to meet a black man or the devil are part of the legend of the blues. As with the crossroads ghosts of Northamptonshire, the night spirits of such places are dangerous to humans, and only the brave, foolhardy, or desperate would venture there. But for those who do, who are not killed or driven mad by the experience, the rewards are great.

Carl Maria von Weber's opera *Der Freischütz,* first performed in 1821 (the English translation is either *The Free-Shooter* or *The Marksman*), tells of the ritual casting of magic bullets at a crossroads, which is part of Central European magical tradition. These magic bullets are infallible: they always hit the target (hence the expression "magic bullet" for a certain quick solution of a problem). In *Der Freischütz,* the protagonist, Kaspar, sings: "Hush! Every moment is precious!" *The moonlight has dwindled to a tiny beam. Kaspar takes the casting ladle.* "Watch me so that you learn the art." *He takes the ingredients out of his hunting bag and throws them in one after another.* "First the lead—some ground glass from broken church windows; you can find that!—Some quicksilver!—Three bullets that have hit their mark! The right eye of a hoopoe, the left one of a lynx! Probatum est! Now the blessing of the bullets!" *He bows to the earth in each of three pauses.* "Protect us, you who watch in darkness! Samiel, Samiel! Give ear! Stand by me in this night Till the spell is complete! Bless for me the herb and lead, Bless them by seven, nine and three, That the bullet be obedient! Samiel, Samiel, to me!"

The crossroads is a metaphor for a place or time where we must make a decision between alternative courses of action. Like casting metal or dice, there is a stark irrevocability of the moment of definition. The random possibilities become determinate immediately after the casting takes place. The crossroads thereby marks the place and time from which there is no turning back.

10

THE MYSTIC TRIANGLE

No-Man's Land

In the West Country magical enclosures are called gallitraps, which folklorist Theo Brown viewed as transdimensional gateways, artificial entrances to the underworld (1966, 125). The name *gallitrap* was given to a magic circle, pentacle, or triangle made by a conjuring parson to lay a ghost or entrap a criminal. An account of ghost laying by an eighteenth-century Cornish conjuring parson named Corker, at Bosava, near Lamorna, refers to a sacred triangle: "The parson, assisted by Dr. Maddron and the miller, drew the magic pentagram and sacred triangle, within which they placed themselves for safety, and commenced the other ceremonies, only known to the learned, which are required for the effectual subjugation of restless spirits . . ." (Rees 1898, 255). A gallitrap also can be a particular kind of "a waste piece of land." They are uncultivated, usually triangular, pieces of ground such as the pieces of ground at a trifinium, the center of the junction of three country roads. This is also called a "cocked hat" (Brown 1966, 124), but more commonly "no-man's land." In the 1930s, C. B. Sibsey noted that in the neighborhood of Frieston in Lincolnshire, "triangular corners of fields are filled with trees; and the groups are known as 'Devil's Holts.' The belief is still current that these were left for the Devil to play in, otherwise he would play in the fields and spoil the crops" (quoted by Rudkin 1934, 250).

Similar eldritch land triangles in other parts of Britain are called the Old Guidman's Ground, the Gudeman's Croft, the Halieman's Ley, the Halyman's Rig, the Black Faulie, Clootie's Croft, and the Devil's Plantation. It was customary for the farmer to promise never to till the earth there (McNeill 1957, I, 62). In his *Letters on Demonology and Witchcraft,* Sir Walter Scott noted, "Though it was not expressly avowed, no one doubted that 'the gudeman's croft' was set apart for some evil being; in fact, that it was the portion of the arch fiend himself . . . this was so general a custom that the Church published an ordinance against it as an impious and blasphemous usage" (1885, 78–79). These uncultivated triangles are no-man's land because they belong to no human but to the denizens of the spirit world.

During the Great War (World War I, from 1914 to 1918) No-Man's Land was a place of death, the battle-torn landscape between the trenches of the opposing armies. It was literally a place of the dead, territory fought in and fought over, to be won or lost yard by yard at the cost of the combatants' blood. The literal destruction of the entire landscape of the front line by shellfire, trench digging, and tunneling made the pre-war French or Flemish place-names meaningless. Bridges and hills were known by numbers only, other features known by letters, like Y Ravine, and places renamed for functions, like Transport Farm. The British soldiers gave the most dangerous places on the front names like Hellblast Corner, Hellfire Corner, and Shrapnel Corner, and roads across devastated territory were given ironic names taken from fashionable streets in London and Edinburgh. Although the places had not been called that pre-war, this was not an imaginary geography but rather a direct, if often cynical, response to a real, deadly situation.

No-Man's Land in France and Belgium was not a flat and featureless place, as it is portrayed in so many movies. It contained all kinds of landscape features too large to be obliterated by constant shellfire. Though they were still called woods, what had been woodland became

Fig. 10.1. Although the armistice was November 11, 1918, the war did not end legally until June 21, 1919, hence my great-grandfather's medal reads "The Great War For Civilisation 1914–1919."

shell-cratered, churned-up ground littered with military debris and tangles of barbed wire as well as the dismembered body parts of the slain, the blasted remnant trunks of trees still standing shattered among the mayhem. Where villages had stood was more rubble and debris, bunkers dug into the remnants of cellars, trenches cut across roads and railway lines with no regard to what had once been there. The utilitarianism of all-out industrialized war overwhelmed everything else. The British cartoon reproduced on page 91, typical of the cynical gallows humor of the time, is a telling indictment of the indiscriminate destruction all around that had reduced a fertile landscape to a featureless wreck.

After World War I a British war graves commission decided that war memorials should be set up in the cities, towns, and villages that had lost men who had died in the war—which was most of them. The names of the fallen were inscribed on the new memorials "lest we forget." In one of those "coincidences" that link hitherto-unconnected places or things, giving them a much deeper symbolic significance (like the Seven Stars), many were set up on triangular plots of land at village road junctions. These triangles were the original "no-man's lands"— called that long before the war changed the meaning of the expression. In many cases the memorials were a reinstatement of the sacred, for many of these sites once had possessed stone crosses, perhaps erected to counter the spirits who dwelled in these eldritch places. Most had been demolished at the Reformation. The war memorials renewed this tradition, for many were contemporary versions of medieval or Celtic standing crosses. Whether or not intentional, the choice of village no-man's

First Contemptible : "D'you remember halting here on the retreat, George?"
Second Ditto : "Can't call it to mind, somehow. Was it that little village in the wood there down by the river, or was it that place with the cathedral and all them factories?"

Fig. 10.2. A World War I cartoon

lands for World War I memorials has a striking symbolism. Because the numbers of the fallen in the numerous wars fought all over the British Empire since the Battle of Waterloo had been relatively low, each war taking a few thousand at most, the number of memorials erected to those wars was insignificant compared with all that were set up after the mass slaughter of the Great War.

Most memorials to the Victorian wars were in the form of individual plaques in churches. But more than a thousand memorials were erected to the fallen of the Second Boer War (1899–1902), and these formed the model for the many more that were set up after the next war. And later the dead of World War II (1939–1945) were commemorated on memorials that had been set up for the first one. Similarly, the dead of wars, skirmishes, and counterinsurgency operations fought by the United Kingdom after World War II—in Korea, Malaya, Kenya, Suez, Cyprus, Aden, Oman, Northern Ireland, the Falklands, Bosnia, Kuwait, Kosovo, Afghanistan, Iraq, and Libya—usually find their names on Great War monuments. The most bizarre of all British war memorials is a 1949 bus shelter at Dunchurch, Warwickshire, far removed from either the horrors of war or the solemn memorialization of the dead by stone crosses, stelae, and cenotaphs.

The triangular corners of English fields called devil's holts and devil's plantations were recalled by Rupert Brooke (1887–1915) in his poem *The Soldier,* where he wrote the following lines made famous by his death in the Great War.

> *If I should die, think only this of me:*
> *That there's some corner of a foreign field*
> *That is for ever England.*

War memorials on land triangles, as well as memorializing the suffering of men in combat zones, serve as places for ceremonies where those attending can feel part of a glorious history that the dead represent. In so doing they invoke the spirits of the dead present in the

Fig. 10.3. Memorial to the
dead of the Great War,
Hills Road, Cambridge

no-man's land through their names inscribed on the war memorial, a
modern version of the magical rites traditionally conducted at crossroads and trifinia.

Monuments, Memory, and Memorials

Back in the 1980s, on my first visit to Stuttgart, Germany, the man I
was staying with took me walking with his dog in the local park. As we
entered it, he pointed out an ordinary-looking patch of grass where, I
was told, a Nazi monument had once been. It no longer existed, he said,
because it had been blown up in 1945 by the French army of occupa-
tion. By telling me, a visitor who had no idea that such a thing had ever
existed there, he was actually maintaining the monument's purpose in a
virtual form. Shortly afterward I met a woman who had just attended a
Roman Catholic pilgrimage in Ipswich. She told me that each year local
Catholics march in a procession to a shoe shop, where they stand in the
street praying and singing hymns. The reason for this is that the shop

occupies the ground where, in medieval days, stood a most holy shrine of Our Lady, the Virgin Mary, which had been destroyed in 1536. In Stuttgart, Ipswich, and all over the world, historical records and local memory keep places alive with meaning even when the physical reminders of that meaning have been obliterated. This happens with both religious and secular monuments, and even with fictional events that never took place.

Most of the intact monuments present in our everyday world are examples of the objectification of place in the service of politics. The most grandiose instances of this are the cities founded to glorify individuals and bearing their names. This is not new: Alexandria is named after the Macedonian king Alexander the Great. In France and America, Saarlouis and Washington commemorated the founders of different "new orders"—being named after the French king Louis XIV and the first president of the United States, George Washington. Renaming does not work in quite the same way, as can be seen with the fates of Leningrad, Stalingrad, Cape Kennedy, and Karl-Marx-Stadt, all restored to their earlier names less than a century after they got new names in honor of political figures. The older names remained in memory and culture, even when the authorities prohibited people from using them. And, paradoxically, the new names, once removed, are still remembered.

The monuments of a demagogue are always obliterated by his successors once his rule has ended. Shortly after the emperor Nero died in the year 68 CE, every monument and building he had constructed in Rome was demolished. The colossal gilded bronze statue Nero had set up to his own glory was taken down, the head cut off, and a new idealized head of the god Apollo set on it. Moved to stand by the Flavian Amphitheatre, the colossus gave the arena its common name, the Coliseum. Rebellions against tyrannical regimes frequently vent themselves on monuments. In 1871, Communard revolutionaries who had taken over Paris pulled down the imperial column in the Place Vendôme, toppling the statue of Napoléon and afterward renaming the square Place Internationale. In 1953 insurrectionary rebels in East Germany smashed statues of Stalin, and in Dublin in the 1950s the damaged plinths of statues were all that remained of monuments to British generals and royalty that had been blown up by members of the Irish Republican Army. This campaign culminated 1966 in the destruction by an IRA bomb of Nelson's Pillar in Dublin's O'Connell Street, a major landmark at the geomantic center of the Irish capital. In later years statues of Lenin and Saddam Hussein have been toppled in front of the cameras. It is the inevitable long-term fate of all monuments.

Other monuments have been demolished or moved for more prosaic, nonpolitical reasons, to facilitate road widening or enable city redevelopment. In the 1960s the enormous memorial to the fallen of the Crimean War that stood on a triangular site at Moorhead at the junction of Furnival Street in the center of Sheffield was demolished during redevelopment. After a century had passed there were few who cared about Queen Victoria's wars. But though the revolutions of time have destroyed many, there are still plenty of grandiose monuments left—in magical terms, on lays on the land—so that we can experience their effect on us today. In the United States the cult of personality has meant that one side of Mount Rushmore is carved into the colossal likenesses of several presidents. In Germany hundreds of Bismarck Towers remain, and more particularly, the even more grandiose monuments of the Kaisers' Second Reich, such as the Kyffhäuserdenkmal and the Völkerschlachtdenkmal at Leipzig.

The geomantic meaning of these inescapable, overwhelming monuments has long been discussed. In London the huge monument to Queen Victoria that was constructed in front of Buckingham Palace at the beginning of the twentieth century has been criticized by visiting Chinese master geomants for disrupting the royal feng shui. Making an analogy with the geomantic principles of the emperor's palace in the Forbidden City in Beijing, some have even suggested that the inauspicious placement of this monument, blocking the Mall, has magically accelerated the decline and fall of the British Empire.

Everyone who encounters such a monument cannot ignore its presence, for by both its significant location and sheer physical size it demands attention. There is no need for memory and the re-creation of the monument in virtual form through local tales or faded photographs at these places. In every country imperial monuments have been designed deliberately to symbolize overwhelming power and domination, creating a sense of national unity at places that have some resonance with national mythology. The enormous Italian National Monument in Rome is a classic example.

But what about the future of these monuments? We are now in a postmodern age when the cult of personality is virtual, through the electronic media, and disputed, through pluralism. Political monuments no longer need to exist in physical reality at all. But there is still felt a need to mark place. New monuments in the British Isles, like the Angel of the North, have been built in an attempt to create a local identity where it seems to be absent. At Wednesbury in the West Midlands, a steel image of Sleipnir, the eight-legged horse of Woden, was set up on a hillside in 1999. This is because Wednesbury was a holy place of the god in Anglo-Saxon pagan times, but the statue was not erected by pagans, though of course they visit it and use it as a location for rituals. The sculpture was actually part of the landscaping around a new tramway, which was actually blessed by the Roman Catholic papal nuncio. In contemporary society no public monument has a single, clear meaning anymore. It is up to the individual to read meaning into it. The remains of rites performed clandestinely by local pagans can be seen at the feet of Sleipnir. But to most people, the eight-legged horse is just a piece of public art with no cultic meaning—just like the shoe shop in Ipswich.

Inevitably, all intact monuments will eventually fall into ruin, like all human artifacts. Although the same word is used to describe both of them, there are two kinds of monuments, whose natures, once separate, have become blurred. Most of those artifacts called "ancient monuments" were not set up to be actual monuments of anything. They are largely ruins that are considered monuments of past times. They have been given the function of monuments. Ruins in the landscape have an appeal to the romantic sentiment, since they embody the inevitable tragic end of all human endeavors. The original intention of the builders to defy nature and time is still visible in the ruin, but its disintegrated condition demonstrates the ultimate failure of this intention.

By definition, ruins are in a state of progressive decay. Unless human action is taken, they will continue to disintegrate until they are utterly destroyed. But because some of the ruins in the landscape are deemed worthy of preservation by those concerned with heritage, they are artificially maintained at the degree of ruin they were at at the time they were taken over for "conservation." Thereafter the ruins are subjects to actions to prevent further decay, keeping them as permanent, fixed ruins halted at a particular, arbitrary stage of disintegration. The reason for this is essentially a romantic aesthetic, the maintained ruin in the landscape being an instance of the picturesque, essentially a version of the eighteenth-century follies, which were new fake ruins built on the estates of the rich at appropriate places to produce intriguing, mysterious, picturesque views.

Those engaged in the conservation/heritage take something that is old, decaying, and in danger of disintegration and attempt to stop the decay, to preserve it for future generations. The ruins are considered worthy of maintenance because they have a social function. They are visited by tourists, are very good for business, and help to bolster certain ideas about local and national history. The ruins are thus transformed into monuments *to* the past rather than being structures *from* the past. These social reasons are, of course, never stated, for they smack of profiteering and propaganda. The fact that the ruins are picturesque, which is the reason they were recognized in the first place and saved from further decay, is also not a utilitarian argument to spend taxpayers' money on them. Instead the conservation is presented as necessary for scientific reasons: archaeology will progress to the point where scientists will be able to determine what these places *really* were for or how they were *really* used. The prime example of this is Stonehenge, the classic maintained ruin. The progression of academic knowledge is the real reason, we are told, for the preservation.

This deconstruction of the conservation/heritage viewpoint does not mean that this author is calling for them to be demolished.

The places should be peremptorily demolished as worthless constructs of present-day obsessions. Most were already gone centuries ago, and that is why the few that remain are valued. In the case of megalithic monuments, land that was cleared of standing stones was a particular kind of landscape where arable farming could be most readily performed. Standing stones were in the way of the plough, and so they were removed and broken up. In most cases stones that were not ripped out of the ground to facilitate ploughing were in marginal land where it was not worth the effort to remove them. So the land where we find such stones has a different appearance from the land without stones. It was this latter land that became celebrated as a certain type of picturesque, spiritual landscape, which led to the preservation of such sites. But it is in a strange situation that we find these ancient structures. In most cases the guardian-conservators see the present as a potential threat. These ruins were saved in the past for posterity, and we, today, are that posterity. But any contemporary use of these preserved ruins is often considered a bad thing by those whose business it is to guard and maintain them. The contested meaning of Stonehenge over the past century is a perfect example of this clash of perceptions.

11

EARTH MYSTERIES
AND MAGIC

Feng Shui and Ley Lines

In the past decades the concept of feng shui has become well established outside China and the Chinese diaspora, even going through a brief period in the 1990s when it was a fashionable element in mainstream interior design. So much so that at the time it was mocked as "the ancient Chinese art of moving furniture." A significant proportion of feng shui practice in the West now is a direct transplant of Chinese artistic forms, which appear exotic in a European context but are sometimes out of place. In any human activity there are underlying principles that are transcendent of the outward form. The many systems of magic that exist in the world are particular cultures' ways of accessing the same powers. One can orient a temple of any tradition—a church, a mosque, or a library—even though the structures' architectural forms may be quite different from one another. The Taoist spiritual principles that underlie much of feng shui are embedded within it; the outward artistic forms of Chinese art are not inevitably part of it. Earlier usages of feng shui in Europe often used the principles without the outward Chinese appearance, which is, of course, a proper way to use them.

Of course there is also an indigenous European art of placement, a tradition that originated more than four thousand years ago. Like feng shui, the European tradition seeks to discover, express, and enhance the essence of the spirit of the place. This intangible quality is described as the genius loci, the spirit of the place. The location of buildings, especially those sacred to the genius loci and the gods, was a matter of great importance in European antiquity. Creating a harmonious attunement to the powers of a place was achieved through the divination techniques of augury. Omens were observed to determine the spiritual suitability of a place for sacred rites, altars, temples, and mausoleums.

Members of the Roman College of Augurs were the masters of this ancient Etruscan art, and the agrimensores, who were practical field surveyors, were schooled in the arts of reading the landscape for its numinous as well as its physical characteristics. Every Roman temple and town was thus located according to the geomantic principles of the Etruscan discipline, not solely according to the price of land or the other considerations that are universal today. After the collapse of the Roman Empire in the West, geomantic practices were maintained in the placement and orientation of churches and in various building traditions maintained by guilds of craftsmen.

During the Renaissance, Roman geometrical techniques were rediscovered and served as the basis for town layout that included straight avenues punctuated by churches, fountains, and monuments. From Rome this tradition spread to the north, where it appeared in the planning for towns as well as parkland around cities and great country palaces such as Versailles (established in 1671) and Kassel (1688). There are examples of this type of placement in early eighteenth-century London in the work of architects James Gibbs and Nicholas Hawksmoor, including the aligned churches in the Strand and the layout of Greenwich with Saint Alfege Church and Saint Anne's Church in Limehouse, across the River Thames, built on the alignment of the Royal Naval Hospital. The city of Karlsruhe in Baden, Germany, founded in January 1715, is the most perfect manifestation of the system. It had thirty-two straight

Fig. 11.1. Sacred geometry Karlsruhe plan, founded 1715
(illustration by Christian Thran, 1729)

roads radiating from the ducal palace tower at its center and churches on insular sites, with some of the lines as parkland avenues. The layout remains to this day. But around the beginning of the eighteenth century, a strong awareness of feng shui was present in the West. It played

Fig. 11.2. Karlsruhe line

an important part in the reaction against straight alignments in the layout of gardens and parkland.

However, feng shui has been around in the West for much longer, since the sixteenth century at the latest, when Jesuit missionaries to China began to bring back accounts and artifacts to Europe. A feng shui compass was exhibited in London as early as 1600. The Danish antiquarian Ole Wurm also owned one, and it was put on show in the Raritatenkabinet in Copenhagen. In 1655, after his death, an engraving of it was published by his son in Leiden in Holland in *Musæum Wormianum* (Golvers 1994, 331–50). In the Latin description of the compass was a description of the eight trigrams. Later books, such as the Reverend Ernest John Eitel's *Feng-Shui, or the Rudiments of Natural Science in China* from 1873, also had relatively detailed descriptions of the compass, so its meaning and function were not unknown in Europe from then onward, though it is clear that the

Compass School was not the main inspiration for European landscape design influenced by feng shui.

In 1685, Sir William Temple wrote an essay, *Upon the Gardens of Epicurus,* in which he referred to irregular planting: "For there may be other forms wholly irregular that may, for aught I know, have more beauty than any of the others; but they must owe it to some extraordinary dispositions of nature in the seat. . . . Something of this I have seen in some places, but heard more of it from others who have lived much among the Chinese; a people, whose way of thinking seems to lie as wide of ours in Europe, as their country does." Temple noted that the Chinese landscape layout was "without any order or disposition of

Fig. 11.3. A feng shui compass

parts that shall be commonly or easily observed: and, though we have hardly any notion of this sort of beauty, yet they have a particular word to express it, and, where they find it hit their eye at first sight, they say the *Sharawadgi* is fine or is admirable."

Temple's essay was the beginning of the reaction against straight-line planning that led to what was called "the English garden," actually the use of feng shui in a European context. In London in 1712, Joseph Addison wrote, "Writers, who have given us an account of *China,* tell us, the Inhabitants of that Country laugh at the Plantations of our *Europeans,* which are laid by the Rule and Line; because, they say, any one may place Trees in equal Rows and uniform Figures. They choose rather to show a Genius in Works of this Nature, and therefore always conceal the art by which they direct themselves" (101–2).

Feng shui influenced the eighteenth-century British landscape gardener and architect Sir William Chambers, who traveled extensively in China and learned the principles of feng shui, which he applied to his gardens and buildings in England. His 1772 book *A Dissertation on Oriental Gardening* contained the principles of feng shui, which British writers since Sir William Temple had called *sharawadgi.* Chambers bewailed the fact that there were no skilled practitioners of the art in Britain: "Is it not singular then, that an Art with which a considerable part of our enjoyments is so universally connected, should have no skilled professors in our quarter of the world?" Chambers's geomantically sited pagoda in Kew Gardens, in southwest London, built of brick rather than timber in 1761, still stands.

The English garden landscape design became so well established by the nineteenth century that its feng shui origin was almost forgotten. By the mid-nineteenth century, writings on feng shui ignored the fact that it had been incorporated into the British landscape for more than a century. Certain ideas of feng shui were assimilated into British culture, even when they were viewed as mild eccentricities. Charles Dickens, who died in 1870, is known to have followed feng shui so that on his travels he always moved his bed into a proper

Fig. 11.4. Kew Gardens pagoda

north–south orientation, wherever he slept (Ackroyd 1990, 222–23). In 1873, Eitel, a Protestant cleric who had been sent as a missionary to China by the London Missionary Society, published his book *Feng-Shui, or the Rudiments of Natural Science in China*. Chapter 4 of his book is titled "The Breath of Nature" (45–54), and in chapter 3 he describes the meanings of the rings on the geomantic compass (33–44). And in 1891, the doyen of the arts and crafts movement, the architect and designer William Richard Lethaby, made reference to aspects of feng shui in his highly influential book *Architecture, Mysticism and Myth.* However, the earlier uses of feng shui in Europe seem to have been unknown to Eitel, Lethaby, and other writers of the period.

In the early twentieth century, articles were published in English on feng shui in China in the *East of Asia Magazine* by Western authors such as Helena von Poseck and James Hutson. Around the same time, leading architects of the arts and crafts movement, including Mackay Hugh Baillie Scott and the Cambridge University professor of architecture Edward Schroeder Prior, were very aware of the location of their buildings, constructed so as to harmonize with their sites and possess a soul (Baillie Scott 1906, 73–75). The mid-twentieth-century British town planner Sir Patrick Abercrombie incorporated some feng shui principles into his work. In 1933, in his book *Town and Country Planning,* Abercrombie quoted a Chinese text that described the planner as a person who was able to reconcile various different elements according to "the local currents of the cosmic breath" (230). He added that while such esoteric principles were not appropriate in their entirety in modern practice, "it should be possible to evolve a system of landscape design which will be authoritative enough to prevent brutal outrage on one hand, and a misguided attempt at bogus naturalism on the other" (232).

When Abercrombie and James Paton Watson redesigned Plymouth's city center following its wartime devastation in 1940 and 1941, it was rebuilt with a completely new street plan based on an axial avenue, a north–south *via sacra* toward the sea called Armada Way that located the main council offices at a place in conformity with feng shui principles. The ancient quarter called the Barbican, which was relatively undamaged, retained its sixteenth-century street plan. According to the commentator David Matless, "Abercrombie presented Feng Shui as a doctrine of intervention, seeking an evolving functional aesthetic harmony between humanity and the environment" (1993, 168). Of course, when built, the new architecture was 1950s concrete modernism, neither traditional Western English nor Chinese in materials or style.

Many of the British landscape architects from the eighteenth to the twentieth centuries fully integrated feng shui into their practice. However, apart from the occasional pagoda, pavilion, or Chinese temple, such as in Peasholm Park in Scarborough, North Yorkshire, where in 1911, Harry W. Smith employed feng shui in the design of a Japanese garden, their work did not look oriental because the essential principles rather than the outward form were followed.

Chinese-style buildings were erected in many eighteenth-century landscapes in Britain. Subsequently, as at Stowe in Buckinghamshire, most of the Chinese-style buildings have been demolished while the European classical ones remain. The largest remaining antique Chinese-style building in Britain is Chambers's pagoda at Kew Gardens.

Fig. 11.5. Peasholm Park, Scarborough

Contemporary new age beliefs absorbed feng shui by a roundabout route. In the mid-1960s there was a renewed interest in the work of Alfred Watkins more than forty years earlier. Watkins was a long-term member of one of those local antiquarian field clubs that existed all over Britain in the era before World War I. The Woolhope Naturalists Field Club was its name, and its members inquired into all things of antiquarian, historical, and scientific interest. The club investigated local phenomena as well as ancient buildings and wildlife, so Watkins was one of the members who wrote a report on the Herefordshire earthquake of 1896. Other reports from Watkins were about the ancient stone crosses and pigeon houses of the county. For his report on the Celtic and later crosses, he visited each of the 120 known and remaining ones, all of which he photographed. This eventually came out in 1929 as a book titled *The Standing Crosses of Herefordshire.*

All of this work, both professional and for his society, was what would be expected of a talented county businessman of his day. But the obsession of his later life, the alignment of ancient sites, was not. In his writings Watkins claimed that his ideas about straight lines on the landscape came entirely from his own experience. An incident recorded in his first book on the subject, *Early British Trackways,* published in 1922, gave the date of his discovery as June 30, 1921. Later, this date was to be celebrated by late-twentieth-century ley hunters at mystics' picnics, moots, and other events. On that day, Watkins recalled, he noticed on a map a straight line joining certain landscape features. With the enthusiasm of the converted, and this comes through in his writing of the event, he suddenly found it yielded "astounding results in all districts, the straight lines to my amazement passing over and over again through the same class of objects." These objects, he surmised, had been "practical sighting points" on the ancient trackways of pre-Roman Britain.

Watkins always claimed this insight to be his own original idea. But subsequent archival research in the 1970s, published by the Institute of Geomantic Research, revealed that Watkins had actually been present

Fig. 11.6. *The Ley Hunter's Manual*
by Alfred Watkins, 1927

at Woolhope Club meetings where the similar ideas of William Henry Black, a Victorian antiquarian who wrote about landscape lines, had been discussed. The idea of hidden lines on the landscape was not so new after all. But what Watkins did that made his work last while his forerunners were forgotten was to give the lines a name: *leys*. Subsequently added to tautologically as ley lines, this word was Watkins's interpretation of an Anglo-Saxon word found in many English place-names, meaning originally "a wood," and later, "a clearing." Watkins interpreted this as meaning a straight line cleared through a wood, though it is probable that many of the villages that he thought lay on straight lines had the place-name suffix *-ley,* such as Didley and Bitterley, as illustrated in his first book.

His major exposition on the subject was a book titled *The Old Straight Track,* published in 1925, and through it the healthy outdoor

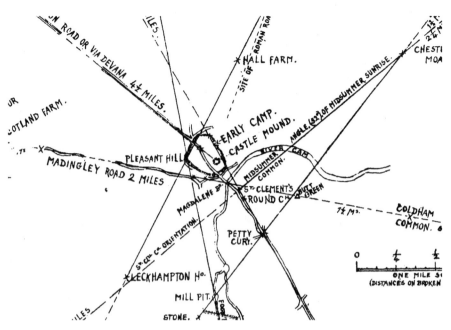

Fig. 11.7. Detail from *The Old Straight Track*
by Alfred Watkins, Cambridge, 1932

sport of ley hunting, an esoteric version of rambling, was born. This was the golden age of the Boy Scouts, the Woodcraft Folk, and the more mystical Kindred of the Kibbo Kift, whose members carried banners showing Stonehenge and other prehistoric British antiquities and celebrated festivals in the countryside, including an althing at Whitsuntide, the post-Easter Pentecost festival, and a gleemote around Lammas, the wheat harvest festival (Ross 2003, 85–98). Members of these groups all enjoyed camping and rambling in the country, and ley hunting fitted in perfectly with the muscular preoccupations of the time. The outbreak of World War II put an end to the rambling, and as Watkins's associates aged, ley hunting dwindled.

But it was the widespread availability of *The Old Straight Track* as late as the 1960s that led to a reawakening of interest in what Watkins had done, and ley hunting was taken up by a new generation. When I founded the Institute of Geomantic Research in 1975, it was only forty years after Watkins's death. The last surviving member of his Straight Track Club, Egerton Sykes, whom I knew, died around the same time. Ley hunting fitted in well with the hippy ethos of the 1960s and '70s. Many began to interpret the British countryside in a spiritual, romantic, way as an authentic place transcendent of all the common utilitarian interpretations, such as development, academic archaeology, or tourism and the heritage industry. Looking for leys in the landscape became a kind of mystical quest akin to Frodo Baggins's mission to get the Ring to Mount Doom in *The Lord of the Rings,* which fired the imaginations of that time. This idea of magical questing later had an important impact on the ethos of many of Great Britain's post-1960s new age travelers (e.g., Hetherington 2000, 127–28).

Watkins was popularly believed to have had a vision of glowing lines across the land, and hippies sitting on top of Glastonbury Tor also saw

Fig. 11.8. Mountain goddess apparition drawing, 2000
(drawing by Nigel Pennick)

them, even if only in drug-fueled reverie. Now again, there was a market for Watkins's idea, even if the interpretation had changed completely from anything the Victorian, free-trade, radical traditionalist county councilor might have meant by them. Two of Watkins's four books on leys, *The Old Straight Track* (1925) and *The Ley Hunter's Manual* (1927) were republished in 1970 and 1977, respectively. Subsequently, dowsers, channelers, and other mystics gave their views of what leys were, and even changed their name—to *ley lines.*

In 1968, in an article in the London underground magazine *Albion* and a year later in his book *The View Over Atlantis,* John Michell linked Watkinsian leys with the *lung mei,* "lines of dragon current" of Chinese Fung-Shui (as it is spelled in the book) (1969, 50–51). Michell suggested that the fertility of the Earth depended on the passage of the dragon flying overhead and down a straight line at certain seasons of the year (63). He also noted that flying saucers (called UFOs now) had a tendency to navigate along straight lines on the Earth's surface (196).

This conflation of dragons, UFOs, and feng shui rapidly captured the imagination of people who rambled the land looking for sacred places and hidden energies or hoping to encounter aliens from another planet. Now British ley lines were no longer seen as prehistoric track-ways, but envisioned as dragon paths or channels of *qi,* the Chinese "energy" dealt with in feng shui. Dowsers, hitherto concerned with finding underground water, lost items, and illnesses in human subjects, took to following what they perceived as subtle energies flowing along ley lines. Even rock musicians got in on the act, with former Genesis guitarist Steve Hillage singing about opening up the old straight tracks and fertilizing the Earth in his 1976 song "Electrick Gypsies."

Ironically, despite this renewed interest, it had been forgotten that only a quarter of a century earlier, Plymouth had been rebuilt on feng shui principles. In what had now been dubbed "Earth mysteries," certain long-distance lines acquired names and a mythos, whether or not they were actually verifiable alignments of ancient sites, as Watkins had defined them. Michell's most famous line, from Saint Michael's Mount on the coast of Cornwall to the east coast "above Lowestoft" (1969, 64; 1983, 72–74), was analyzed by Michael Behrend in 1975. Behrend demonstrated mathematically that some places on it were "several hundred metres" away from a true straight line (1975, 1). But his discovery was largely ignored. The Saint Michael Line, as it became known, was too good an idea to abandon on the grounds that it was not actually a straight line, the finding of which ley hunting was all about. In this heyday of geomantic research, mathematics played an important role, for some claimed that many, if not all, such lines detected on maps were artifacts of mathematical randomness (e.g., Forrest 1976). But the idea of long straight lines hidden in the landscape was so attractive that "earth energies" were soon attached to them, and the original idea and its history were discounted or forgotten as inconvenient. A whole new edifice of beliefs was built on the idea of energy lines, and if Watkins could reemerge from the shades now and look on what people have made of his idea, it is clear that he would be shocked. But such is the way of ideas and their founders.

12

THE FAIRGROUND
A Magical Space

Yorkshire has its feasts; other counties their wakes; and Norfolk its fairs.

WILLIAM MARSHALL,
THE RURAL ECONOMY OF NORFOLK, 1787

Fairs are part of our tradition of "keeping up the day." Special days of the year are times of celebration and festivity. Many British medieval fairs were held on saints' days, such as Saint Giles's Fair in Oxford and Bartholomew Fair at Smithfield in London. Other special days celebrated by fairs included the Pack Monday Fair at Sherborne, held on the Monday after Old Michaelmas, and the Southwold Fair on the three days following Holy Trinity. The Midsummer Fair at Cambridge, conducted every year since 1211 in an unbroken continuity, celebrates the summer solstice. Midsummer Common, on which the fair is held, once had a holy well, Barnwell, which was visited at the solstice for the performance of popular sports such as boxing, wrestling, and foot and horse racing. Fairs even have their own traditional songs with unique tunes, such as "Copshawholme Fair," "Brigg

Fair," "Thame Fair," and the most famous of all, "Scarborough Fair." The Furry Dance at Helston, Cornwall, held in early May each year, was associated with a fair.

Many fairs took place at the times of year when certain produce or commodities were ready for sale. There were horse fairs, sheep fairs, goose fairs, hop fairs, onion fairs, and statute or mop fairs (for hiring people to work). Some fairs, while not solely for the sale and purchase of certain items, were known for special things sold at them, so they were named after them, such as the gingerbread fairs at Birmingham. The Sloe Fair at Chichester was called that because it was held in a field whose entrance was guarded by a notable blackthorn (sloe) tree (Drake-Carnell 1938, 65).

The layout of medieval fairs was deliberate and planned. At the center—the fair's omphalos—was a wooden pole that bore an emblem of authority: a glove, a wooden hand, or the coat of arms of the local lord or king. At Sturbridge, near Cambridge, the post was called a Maypole even though the fair was held each September. Ritually, setting up a fair was conducted in the same manner as founding a new town. Digging a hole at the center, placing certain objects in it as a foundation sacrifice, and the erection of the pole in it were the ceremonial statements that the town had been founded. On the pole were the symbols of authority. Around the post the town was laid out in a rectilinear grid.

The royal hand or glove atop the pole gave rise to the expression "the glove is up!" meaning the fair had begun. Francis John Drake-Carnell tells how at Honiton in Devon in 1937, the fair was begun with an announcement by the town crier, who carried a staff surmounted by a gilt glove:

> *Oyez! Oyez! Oyez!*
> *The Glove is up and the Fair has begun*
> *No man shall be arrested*
> *Until the glove is taken down.*
> *God save the King!"*
>
> (1938, 62–63)

Once the glove was up, everything within the boundary of the fair was under "the King's Peace." Jurisdiction was overseen by a special court, the Court of Pie Powder (from the French *pied poudreux,* "dusty feet"), while stall holders' and traders' tolls were collected by the Tolsey Court (Drake-Carnell, 1938, 45). These courts meted out summary justice to wrongdoers, who were set immediately in the stocks or the pillory or sent to the whipping post. Some of these ancient courts continued into the twentieth century, at Sturbridge until its end in 1932 and at Newcastle-upon-Tyne, Guildford, Ely, and Bristol until the beginning of World War II.

Like the founded towns, the layout of fairs was in grid form, with parallel rows of stalls or booths lined up on either side of the "streets." Each trade or craft was allocated its own row where work could be carried out, making items and selling them. These rows of stalls or booths were set up in the same place each year, and in some places they were replaced with permanent buildings. In the east of Cambridge, the site of the Sturbridge Fair has a grid of streets that follow some of the original fair rows. They are Mercers' Row, Garlic Row, and Oyster Row, which retain their original names, as well as Cheddar's Lane, Stanley Road, and Swann's Road. Although the fair declined and in 1933 was closed down, the Oyster House remained as a public house built on Garlic Row in the years when the temporary rows of the fair became streets with permanent buildings. In later years the Oyster House became the center of activities for carousing, with local musicians playing for dancing on the upper floor. The pub finally closed in 1957 and was finally demolished in 1960. (For details of this important fair and its traditional culture, see appendix 2, "The Sturbridge Fair and the Oyster House Project.")

As commerce altered, fairs became funfairs, and the profession of the traveling showman emerged. Most fairs gradually altered in character until they became only funfairs, complete with mechanical rides, sideshows, and amplified recorded music, but with no more stalls selling commodities. But the tradition of their layout continued into modern times. The technique was revealed in the account of the funeral of "the King of the Showmen," Patrick Collins, at Bloxwich in 1943, which saw his son select the site for his grave with a rite used to determine the center point of a showground (see pages 78–79). The place is marked with the heel with the ritual words "This is the spot." This showman's rite is to indicate where the principal attraction, usually the biggest of the merry-go-rounds, is to be erected. Collins "never measured the ground, but the chosen spot was always in the exact centre of the show-ground" (*Sunday Express,* December 12, 1943). The connection between the center of the fairground, the pole of medieval fairs, and the rotating merry-go-round appears significant. Even if it is coincidental, it is a meaningful link, once recognized.

A few fairs attended by Gypsies (Roma) for horse trading were not subsumed into the funfair culture. The Appleby Horse Fair is the most celebrated of these. But in parallel with the sanctioned charter and statute fairs, there had always been local get-togethers that were unauthorized and unlicensed by the authorities. In the medieval period and onward, scot-ales were held outside the jurisdiction of towns and ecclesiastical authority for the purpose of drinking ale and having a good time. The word *scot* is from the Old English *sceotan,* "to pay" or "contribute": everyone had to pay their way. Scot-ales were held in the forest, on marginal or disputed land, on extraterritorial ground, or other luminal places difficult of access and of dubious jurisdiction— places not subject to common law (Wykes 1979, 36). Games and sports were conducted on common land, on hilltops, in stone circles, and at holy wells on important days of the year, such as May Day, Whitsun, Midsummer, and Lammas.

Stonehenge was one such place where sports were contested. For example, in early July 1781, the following advertisement appeared in the *Salisbury and Winchester Journal:*

On Wednesday the 4th of July instant will be run a race by six young men in sacks over Stonehenge Down for a hat of 10s 6d value.

The same day eleven pair of gloves will be played for at cricket. The wickets to be pitched by nine o'clock. Likewise a new pair of buckskin breeches to be wrestled for . . . he that gets the most pins in three bowls, to have the hat . . . Second day's sport. A cricket match . . . a good hat to be wrestled for, and a fine hat, value one pound, to be bowled for.

A stall selling liquor was provided for the participants' and spectators' refreshments. In later years Stonehenge became a place to be visited by people from farther away, either as a pilgrimage or as a place to meet others and have a good time. Druids started to visit Stonehenge in 1905 (on August 24), and afterward they became the defining feature of the solstice celebrations there. By the time cars were widely available in the 1920s, Stonehenge became the site of jazz parties, with revelers vying with somber Druids waiting for sunup on the summer solstice. And fifty years later, Stonehenge was the focus of a free festival as well as Druidism, pagan spirituality, and conflict with the police.

Fig. 12.1. Stonehenge trilithons

A parallel with commercial sports events, outdoor music festivals began in the 1950s, with jazz being played at stately homes, places like Beaulieu. Later the folk festivals at Sidmouth and Cambridge followed the lead of the jazz lovers, then pop, and even later, rock festivals that modeled themselves initially on the festivals at Monterey and Woodstock in the United States. These were all commercial festivals that charged admission and provided, in theory, facilities for visitors. These jazz and folk festivals had neither geomantic layout nor a mystical dimension, but the influence of the Earth mysteries movement on what became known as the free festivals was apparent.

Free festivals, which grew from the rock and pop music worlds, were not fairs in the traditional sense, but they took from them many of their carnivalesque elements. They emerged as a countercultural response to the commercial festivals such as the Isle of Wight in 1970 (where Jimi Hendrix played "God Save the Queen"). These were seen, in the parlance of the time, as a rip-off, festivals staged by profiteers for their own gain and not for the common good. As they emerged, free festivals were an attempt to stage events with no admission charge, run on a nonprofit basis. Festivals took place in many places on a small scale, and policing was low-key or absent. At Cambridge they were held on Grantchester Meadows and Coldhams' Common. The festival at Glastonbury, now a highly profitable commercial venture, began in 1971 as a free festival, located, it was claimed, on ley lines that intersected at a place where a stage in the form of a pyramid was duly erected to tap the energies. The mystical dimension of this festival was overt, for it drew on a number of esoteric currents: the ancient Celtic Christian mystique of Glastonbury, the landscape zodiac that the early twentieth-century British artist and sculptor Katherine Maltwood described, and Watkinsian leys in their modern guise as lines of subtle energy.

Stonehenge was not the site of free festivals in the early 1970s, though visiting for the summer solstice became increasingly popular. However, the People's Free Festival began in 1972 in Windsor Great Park, part of a royal estate. In 1972 and 1973 the authorities allowed it to take place, but in 1974 they decided to meet it with a large police presence, and it was suppressed with force and many arrests. In 1975 the government offered the People's Free Festival a site on the abandoned airfield at Watchfield. But this was a one-off. In 1974 a group of escapees from the Windsor debacle decamped to Stonehenge, where they had a small festival. The year after that, the Stonehenge Festival assumed the mantle of the People's Free Festival, and increasing numbers of people attended it until by 1984, the last year it was tolerated, it was estimated that fifty thousand people were there. In 1985, Stonehenge was blockaded by police and army units, and the convoy of new age travelers on the way there were ambushed at Cholderton by riot police, with considerable violence (Stone 1996, 153–60). So ended the Stonehenge Festival. For fifteen years after that, the police set up an exclusion zone for four miles around Stonehenge every summer to keep revelers and worshippers away. Only in 2000 was the ban relaxed and people allowed back in to witness the solstitial sunrise.

A series of successful new fairs were staged in East Anglia in the 1970s and 1980s, beginning with the celebrated Barsham Fair of 1972. Subsequent fairs in Norfolk and Suffolk were organized by a number of groups: the East Anglian Arts Trust, Norfolk and Norwich Arts, Albion Fairs, the Stour Valley Collective, and Green Deserts (Barnes 1983, 6–8). In Cambridgeshire, inspired by Barsham, was the Strawberry Fair at Cambridge, held on the traditional fairground of Midsummer Common, which was independent of the other groups. These fairs were seen by the organizers and participants as an authentic expression of local folk culture: "East Anglia has many vital relationships with the history of festival and its objects, and the real Norfolk traditional art is not water-color painting but the practice of festival" (94). The totem used by Albion Fairs was a sunrise motif taken from the radiator pattern of Albion trucks and buses, built in Scotland from 1899 until 1980, another instance of one tradition becoming absorbed and transformed by another (Brown 1982, 7–9; Barnes 1983, 99, 105, 143). Many of these fairs featured geomantic and mystical elements, including mazes

Fig. 12.2. Barsham Fair poster, 1974

Fig. 12.3. Albion Fair poster

Fig. 12.4. Strawberry Fair labyrinth built by Nigel Pennick

and labyrinths, zodiacs, Celtic ogham tree circles, as well as meditation and spiritual rituals. The physical aspects were not for show but rather for performance, dance, and ritual. Those who made and used them were the creators of new magical spaces. Once the fair was over, they were gone.

In that period I was an active participant in the fairs at Rougham, Suffolk, and Lyng, Norfolk, as well as being the designer of the original poster advertising the first Strawberry Fair in Cambridge. In addition to giving talks, being an occasional performer at the multimedia tent, and appearing with the Northstow Mummers, I also was responsible for the geomantic layout, used for several years, of the Green Area at the Strawberry Fair in Cambridge, including a biodegradable labyrinth of sawdust. As Anna Lockwood put it in *Grapevine** in 1983, the fairs

---

**Grapevine was a small magazine. I am quoting from the compilation edited by Richard Barnes (1983, 42).

were viewed as "a viable alternative to an otherwise stagnant and passive social situation, offering a source and more important, an opportunity of active participation for the individual . . . they become for a short time a family, working with the aim of creating that magic of co-operative and shared experience when men forget their pasts and their expectations for the future and just *are!!*" Free fairs and festivals clearly have a place in the contemporary era, especially those that do not follow the model of commercialization and marketing that has pervaded every element of society now, but as ever, when they do take place, they are always under threat from those who see their participants as questioning the everyday—a threat to the public order that must be controlled.

13

ARCHAEOLOGY, TOURISM, AND THE ELDRITCH

It is commonplace today that archaeologists can enter and violate places of ancient sanctity with impunity in their quest for knowledge. They have dug beneath the medieval church of Saint Dionysius in Esslingen, Germany, uprooted the Urnes Stave Church in Norway, burrowed beneath the church of Saint Mary Woolnoth in London and York Minster cathedral in England, and even under the holy of holies of Roman Catholicism, Saint Peter's Basilica in Rome. All of these, and many other churches, are currently consecrated places of worship, where the dead of generations are buried. Many stand at places that were considered sacred by people with other spiritual paths long before organized religion appropriated them. Traditionally the sacred rites of passage of the community are celebrated within these places, as they have been for perhaps thousands of years. Generations of devotees have sought solace and strength in their faith on these holy grounds. Generations of priestesses and priests have conducted the proper sacred rites for them at the correct times. They are sanctuaries, places of true spiritual power. But in so many cases, the implications of this history seem to matter not at all. In their search for

Fig. 13.1. Long Man of Wilmington, Sussex, England

information, unknown artifacts, and the furtherance of their careers, archaeologists have obtained the opportunity to dig within sacred grounds, and they do.

Perhaps this violation of the sacred originated centuries ago with the excavation of the abandoned holy places of Egyptian religion. The guardians of those holy places were long dead when archaeology was invented, and the places were shunned or defaced by the dominant religion, Islam, and the Ottoman imperial masters of the land, who made some baksheesh by granting licenses to dig. Later, imperial agents and settlers in colonial lands dug into the holy places of the natives whom they had subjugated or exterminated. The natives were in no position to object, and the results of this plundering still echo through the law courts today. Following the precedent set by the excavation of shrines of extinct religions and native sacred places, it was only a matter of time before the archaeologists turned their attention to the sacred places of their own culture within their own lands.

Any idea that to disturb the earth beneath these and other venerable buildings might have an effect on their sacredness seems to have been dismissed, even if it was given any thought in the first place. The diggings are authorized because the archaeologists have actually been given permission by the very priests who are the guardians of these sacred places. This profaning of sacred ground is not really the fault of the archaeologists, whose task it is to dig the earth for meaningful remains. It is the priesthood, which is supposed to be the repository of traditional understanding that permits these grounds to be violated. If they would only refuse, then not a gram of sacred earth would be moved. More than anything else, the acquiescence of the priesthood to the archaeologists' demands demonstrates a failure of faith in the traditional understanding of sanctuary.

Because archaeology is a scientific discipline, it views all places and artifacts neutrally. The value placed on a sacred place by a devotee cannot be taken into account, except as an area of socio-geographical study. Even the bones of the dead, who were once living beings like you and me, are no more than material remains to be hauled out from their resting place and taken to a laboratory for scientific analysis. But on a human level, the removal of one's ancestors' bones to a museum (or a labeled cardboard box in the museum basement) is at best an indignity, at worst a sacrilege. Who would not feel outraged if an archaeologist dug up one's grandmother just to put her skull on show in a museum cabinet? But when this is an ancestor from ten generations or more back in time, it does not seem to matter. To those few religious people who still have a sensibility for the holy, to dig in holy ground is equally outrageous (though, of course, fanatics will rejoice if it is the holy ground of a rival religion that is desecrated).

The fact that archaeologists can dig beneath churches and take away foundation deposits, the bones of saints and laity alike, demonstrates that, in general, the clergy as a profession is no longer aware that any difference can be made by doing so. This seems to be the case, because in many churches the priests have actually removed the relics from view so that tourists can see the building more easily. A sad example is the Cathedral of Florence, where the reliquaries and their contents are now in a museum rather than serving as foci for a form of religious devotion within a tradition that goes back for 1,600 years. Now they are there to be viewed only as curios—or high art. Whatever spiritual virtue they contain is discounted. When the little things are no longer held to be sacred, then also are the greatest.

Geomantically, digging away beneath churches profoundly alters the ground on which the building stands. Whether or not the original church was built on the site of a pagan temple whose site was divined

Fig. 13.2. Reliquary of Saint Catherine of Siena, Venice, Italy

by an augur or a sibyl, it was certainly founded with rites and ceremonies that served to empower the building with spirit. Geomancy teaches that there are subtle forces in every place and that at those with particular qualities, sacred places have come into being. It is clear from the wealth of traditional lore across the whole of Europe that churches are such places. In the past witches and magicians as well as priests availed themselves of these powers, for it was a given that they were places of power. If the sacred is not just a human construct, as some argue, but actually emanates from the power within the earth at particular places, then to dig there without the traditional geomantic precautions runs the risk of destroying that power. Those who dig, and those who give them permission to dig, either do not know this or do not think it is a worthwhile tradition to maintain. Either way, the special nature of the earth at that place is forever violated and altered irrevocably.

The inviolable nature of sacred places was formerly enshrined in law. It was recognized that shrines, churches, and graveyards could not be interfered with for any reason. In former times the Free Miners of the Forest of Dean, on the borders of England and Wales, were allowed to dig on any land except the King's Highway, orchards, and churchyards. This right was a continuation of the ancient Celtic tradition of the three classes of sacred places. To violate a churchyard to mine coal was unthinkable. But today archaeologists can and do mine the bones of the dead in churchyards. Once tradition, founded on a spiritual as well as a practical understanding of being, is lost, then all is profaned, and the holy disappears. The spiritually empty, desacralized dereliction of disused parts of cities and the characterless SLOAP (space left over after planning) between apartment high-rises and around motorways and industrial estates has become the characteristic landscape of so many places, reflecting the inner wasteland of the mind-set that produced them.

Places associated with legend are vulnerable to alteration to accommodate the perceived needs of tourism. One such place is connected with the tale of the Lambton Worm, which is the most celebrated dragon legend of Northumbria. The legend tells how, once upon a time, on a Sunday, Lord Lambton was fishing in the River Wear, when he caught not a fish but a weird worm. He rejected it as a worthless catch and threw it down a well by the riverbank. A local woman returning from church asked his lordship if he had caught anything, and he replied, "Why, truly, I think I've caught the Devil," for it was weird, looking something like a newt with nine holes on each side of its head. He told her to look down the well, and she prophesied, "No good will come of it." In the well the worm grew huge and devastated the countryside until the lord, who had returned after pilgrimage to Jerusalem, was forced to fight and kill it.

The locus of this story, Worm Well, was famous locally for another reason, for it was resorted to ceremonially each Midsummer Eve as a wishing well. Sometime after 1840 the well surroundings were

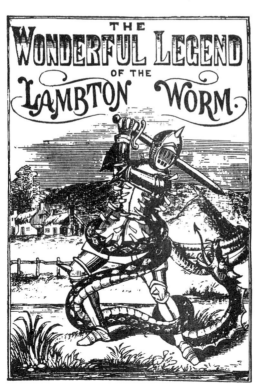

Fig. 13.3. Lambton Worm, 1875

demolished, but in the 1970s a new well was made as a local attraction, for it was deemed a tourist magnet. But because the Washington Development Corporation deemed the real well to be too close to the river's edge, it was identified as a potential danger to visitors, so for health and safety reasons, a replica well was built on another site, much farther from the River Wear, and water supplied to it by a pipe.

Not only holy wells get moved. An archaeologist friend told me in 2010 that she had been traveling in Scotland with a group of people studying Neolithic monuments. Among other ancient structures in the landscape north of Edinburgh, they visited two stone circles. It turned out that the two stone circles had each been moved recently to new sites. The excuse for moving them was that they were in the way of new roads—as if the planners could not route their new roads to avoid archaic structures like stone circles. The first road had been built, but the second one had been canceled, so the stone circle had been moved for nothing. But that is not all. The questioner asked the person in charge whether the original orientation of the stone circle had been reproduced at its new site, only to receive the response that an interest in orientation is "the lunatic fringe of archaeology."

So it appears that the orientation was not maintained when the uprooted stones were set up again in a different place. When an ancient structure is moved, although its physical materials and form remain, its geomantic essence is destroyed. Once it is taken from the place for which it was designed, its place in the landscape, its alignments to hilltops and mountain peaks, its subtle relationship to the geology and watercourses, are all altered. The intentions of the people who put it in its proper place originally are obliterated.

Unfortunately, moving ancient monuments unthinkingly is not a new phenomenon. The London church of Saint Mary Aldermanbury was designed by Sir Christopher Wren to replace an earlier church on the same place that had been burned in the Great Fire of 1666. In the seventeenth century Wren and his associates took great care to design their churches to suit their locations and oriented them according to tradition. In World War II, in the Blitz, the church of Saint Mary Aldermanbury was hit by a bomb and burned out. After standing as a ruin for more than ten years, it was demolished, stone by numbered stone, and shipped to the United States, where it was reconstructed in Fulton, Missouri. This was so it could be rededicated as a memorial to a speech made there by Sir Winston Churchill in which the words *iron curtain* first appeared. The church stands there today, out of place in a context in which it was never designed to be. There are the same problems of new local qualities and orientation as with the stone circles in Scotland.

For several hundred years remains of ancient buildings have been collected by museums and transported to cities where they have been put on show. Whole temples from ancient Egypt, the Hellennic world, Etruria, and the Roman Empire can be visited inside museums in places far from their places of origin. By definition these once-holy buildings, founded by particular rites and ceremonies on places divined by augurs and visited for centuries by devout worshippers, are now items in the museum catalogue, larger versions of the small things seen in glass cases. Their original function as receptacles of the genius loci is long since gone. The places where they once stood have been put to other uses, and even if they are remembered at all as sacred places, they are no longer used as such. In this manner the desacralization of the world progresses.

Parallel to this is the blurring of the distinction between the authentic and the replica. External replicas of holy places have long been made in theme parks. Walt Disney, the inventor of theme parks, was a master of illusion. He knew that external appearances would attract customers, so he filled his parks with concrete and plastic structures that looked like Bavarian castles and medieval towns. Like his cartoons, Disney's buildings were caricatures of the real buildings they purported to be. But his customers knew no different and flocked to the theme parks. So when a stone circle no longer stands where it had stood for four thousand years but is at a new place in a park, however well it has been reerected, it is also no longer distinguishable from a replica.

POSTSCRIPT

Who works not for his fellows starves his soul. His thoughts grow poor and dwindle and his heart grudges each beat, as misers do the dole.

EDGAR WOOD

We are where we are where we are where we are. The situation here and now is the only one we are in. The landscape we live in and visit is a physical and social reality that we have to accept. Magic is not fixed in a particular period of history; neither does it have to be performed at fixed places. Nor is it defined by narrow parameters of spirits, conjuration, paraphernalia, and incantations. Magic of all forms is a living, dynamic system intended for use, not preservation as a museum piece and neither to be made into a spectacle of reenactment. It can exist at any place that is congenial to it, especially those places where negative influences are minimal. In magic, as well as other elements of culture, there are, of course, systems that we call traditions, which were recognized at a particular time in history. But these are all just particular cultural adaptations for accessing the same powers. So today we can talk about (and practice), among others, West Country, East Anglian, Northumbrian, Manx, Welsh, or Icelandic magic; classical Judeo-Christian magic; the magic taught by Heinrich Cornelius Agrippa and his followers; the magic of the black books; Golden Dawn magic; magical systems of modern practitioners; ancient and modern rune magic; hoodoo, Obeah, and Taoist magic; and more. In geomancy too, in parallel, there are many cultural systems: the Etruscan discipline, feng shui, yattara, vastuvidya, vintana, and more.

To classify them, these systems are all viewed through the cultural lenses of the places or cultures from which they originated, that is to say, the places and times where they were recognized as or stated to be coherent systems by experts or commentators. Much of the knowledge and practices of these systems have been available publicly since the nineteenth century; subsequent collectors and investigators during the twentieth century detected or developed further components and made them available. And today the internet enables one to find information on any magical system published there. We are no longer living in a place or time where we are restricted to local knowledge and what we have been taught individually on a one-to-one basis. We have a plethora of sources from which to choose. Of course, one may have aesthetic reasons for practicing one or another of these magical systems: personal preference, feeling part of a particular group, or being a regional resident or member of an ethnic group. Chaos magic emerged from the current milieu where traditions and practices from many sources are equally available. It is a magic that deals with particular things or places in ways that are considered most appropriate to them, not following a particular cultural current. The essence, rather than the form, is deemed the most important thing.

There is a strong wish by anyone who studies the cultures of the past to take the fragments we possess and attempt to piece them together to make a whole. This book may be seen in that way, but it is not my intention. The piecing together of something broken is a procedure that can be done with a pot found in an archaeological dig, so long as all the pieces remain, but it does not work with human culture. However, there is a strong assumption in many quarters that in any aspect of past culture there *is* a whole, like a pot, currently broken into fragments, that can be pieced together again to restore an integrated structure. But this assumption begs the question: What is the whole that we are attempting to reconstruct? There is no cultural whole of anything we may choose to examine that existed at any one time. If we look at the present, can we define the "whole" of any part of culture that may appear to be a category or unit? What is the whole of Great Britain at the moment you read this? The whole of art? It's impossible to answer, because the question, and the nature of the data required, is indeterminate in meaning.

Beliefs that there can be—*should* be—unequivocal and transparent forms of reality, manifested as correct culture, are clearly false. But there is a common belief in every sphere of human activity that there *is* one and only one correct interpretation, which is the final and exact truth. In this absolutist view of reality, all else is error. This is the worldview underlying the principle of the infallibility of the pope and the unchallengeable assertions of many other belief systems that came before and after that particular office was invented. Religions that have a written liturgy, or equally, a fully scored opera, may appear to have a coherence that defines every parameter of how they should be performed. But the nature of each subsequent performance of such scripted cultural events means that is different from the previous one. Nothing can be identical with anything else, even if it is an exact replica, for it is a second example of whatever is being reproduced.

Even the broken pot that is pieced together by the archaeological reconstructors is whole again because of an action different from that which made it originally. The object has a history, even if it cannot be retold. The incidents that resulted in the pot being broken and buried and the incidents of it being dug up and pieced together are all part of its history. In the museum, however, the pot is presented as an object without any of this history; it becomes an ahistorical object, which, if famous, is called an "iconic piece." The values and honor put on these pieces—old, reconstructed, and new—are as much a form of magic as the actions of any conjuring parsons of the past. Magic is a dynamic reordering of present realities to create new situations. As they say in East Anglia, "No door is closed to a toadman."

FINIS

APPENDIX I

GLOSSARY OF TERMS

Abred (Welsh): The Earth, the middle level of the cosmic axis (q.v.).

Albion: An ancient name for the island of Great Britain.

Annwn (Welsh): The underworld, lowest level of the cosmic axis (q.v.).

archetype: The pattern or model on which actual things appear to be formed.

Backbone: British microwave telecommunications system designed for use in and after a nuclear war.

Baneluca: The spiritual boundary around medieval Bury St. Edmunds, Suffolk.

Berlin Wall: A wall built in 1961 around West Berlin by the communist authorities of East Germany. Demolished in 1989.

bonesman: A member of a secret society, the Ancient Order of Bonesmen, associated with gravediggers and graveyard magic.

cardo: The straight north–south road of the Etruscan discipline, crossing the east–west road, the decumanus (q.v.), at the omphalos (q.v.), or center.

carfax: Crossroads that is the geomantic center of a town.

centuriation: Roman system of dividing the land up in a rectilinear grid.

Ceugant (Welsh): The upper level of the cosmic axis (q.v.).

Communard: A member or supporter of the Paris Commune, a revolutionary government that ran the city from March 18 to May 28, 1871, then suppressed by the French army, with seventeen thousand civilian deaths.

conjuring parson: Clergyman with the abilities and powers to lay ghosts and banish spirits.

cosmic axis: The conceptual line linking the three levels of flat-Earth cosmology: the upperworld, middleworld, and underworld.

Daddy: A byname of the devil.

decumanus: The straight east–west road of the Etruscan Discipline, crossing the cardo (q.v.) at the omphalos (q.v.), or center.

desacralization: The process of destroying the quality of sacredness, especially in the landscape.

De Stijl (Dutch): "The style," an art movement founded in 1917 based on spiritual order expressed through rectilinear geometry and dynamic relationships of spatial planes.

electional astrology: Working out the optimal inceptional horoscope for a project in advance and founding the venture at that moment thus determined (the punctual time).

ensouled: Possessing a soul.

Etruscan Discipline: The ancient geomantic system of the Etruscans.

felo de se: Self-murder, suicide.

feng shui (Chinese): Literally, "wind-water"; Chinese geomancy dealing with subtle forces and forms in the landscape.

flying saucer: (see UFO).

foundation: The act of marking the beginning of a building by laying a stone with rites and ceremonies.

genius loci: The spirit of a place.

geomancy: The art of locating buildings and other structures holistically in recognition of the site and the prevailing conditions, physical and spiritual.

glímalgaldur: Icelandic magic using runic talismans for winning at wrestling.

Infallibility of the Pope: A Roman Catholic doctrine that the pope, the head of the church, is always correct when he rules on matters of doctrine.

Iron Curtain: The imagined but agreed-upon border across Central Europe dividing communist countries under Soviet control from the countries of Western Europe.

landvættir (Norse): "Land wights," spiritual beings of the land, Icelandic equivalent to elves, sprites, or fairies.

ley: Straight in the landscape, linking categories of ancient sites defined by Alfred Watkins (1855–1935).

ley hunting: The pastime of searching for leys.

ley line: Landscape line, derived originally from Watkins's concept of leys, but usually claimed to carry subtle energies and sometimes not straight.

locus terribilis: Literally, "terrible place," a place of spiritual terror and danger where humans ought not to venture.

lunatic fringe of archaeology: Name given in the 1970s by Glyn Daniel, professor of archaeology at Cambridge University, to ley hunters, geomantic researchers, and other students and practitioners of Earth mysteries.

magic circle: A circle drawn ritually by a magician to protect him or her from called-up spirits.

materia magica: Materials used in the physical enabling of magic.

meridional: North–south, from the meridian, the middle of the day, noon, when the sun stands in the south.

moot (Anglo-Saxon): A meeting for the purposes of discussion, a council, an Earth mysteries or pagan meeting.

Mundus: The underworld, or its entrance beneath the omphalos (q.v.). In the Etruscan discipline, the Mundus is symbolic of the dwelling place of the Inferiæ, the gods of the underworld.

omphalos: The "navel of the world," spiritual center point, often depicted as an egg stone.

orientation: The deliberate alignment of something with a particular direction. Originally, orientation meant facing toward the east (the Orient), but it now means facing any particular direction.

Ostentarian: The Etruscan magical books, otherwise called the *Libri Tagetici,* which recorded the teachings and practices of the Etruscan discipline.

ostentum (pl. ostenta): An unusual event recognized to be a sign requiring action.

punctual time: The exact moment for a foundation according to electional astrology.

Red Sea: Final place of disposal of banished spirits.

relic: In the Catholic Church, human body part from a saint, used for liturgical and magical purposes.

Royal Roads: In the Celtic tradition certain main roads in Britain and Ireland were designated "Royal." They were extensions of the King's Peace, and travelers on them were protected by special laws.

Saith Seren Y Gogledd (Welsh): The Seven Stars of the North, the constellation of Ursa Major, the Plough, or the Big Dipper.

Seven Stars: The Seven Stars of the North form the constellation of

Ursa Major, the Plough, or the Big Dipper; the Pleiades or Seven Sisters are also known sometimes by this name.

Scutum Davidis: "The Shield of David," a talisman inscribed with a hexagram, the Star of David.

solstices: The shortest and the longest days of the year.

Temenos: The sacred area around a grove, temple, or church.

toadman (or toadwoman): A person who has "been to the river" and performed the toad-bone ritual.

toadmanry: The practices and magical arts of a toadman or toadwoman.

UFO: Acronym for unidentified flying object, a term devised in the 1940s by the United States Air Force to describe unidentified lights and radar traces detected during flying operations and suspected or feared to have a Soviet origin. The term is also used loosely to refer to supposed alien spacecraft from other solar systems, having superseded the earlier term "flying saucer."

wildfolk: The "little people," fairies.

Yggdrasil: The World Tree of the Northern Tradition, the cosmic axis (q.v.).

APPENDIX 2

THE STURBRIDGE FAIR AND THE OYSTER HOUSE PROJECT

In its heyday, the Sturbridge Fair in the suburb of Barnwell, near Cambridge, was one of the largest in Great Britain. Its legacy lives today in the other great Cambridge fair, the Midsummer Fair on Midsummer Common. The Sturbridge Fair was given a charter in 1211 in the reign of King John. The fair's time was defined by the harvest season, being proclaimed on September the seventh of each year, and after the change of the calendar to New Style in 1752, the sixteenth. Even if the harvest had not been gathered, the stallholders were permitted to set up on the unharvested crops. In the center of the main square of the fair, a place called the Duddery, a large Maypole was set up for the duration of the fair. On the final day of the fair, sports such as horse racing, running, wrestling, and boxing took place. On Michaelmas Day at noon, the ploughmen were permitted to enter and begin ploughing up the common, whether or not the last stall keepers had packed up and left. Anything not taken away by then was forfeit to the farmers.

The Sturbridge Fair was a magnet for performers of all kinds, including singers, musicians, and dancers, and for the performance of plays and puppet shows. Gamblers, quack doctors, mountebanks, fortune-tellers, and prostitutes vied for the punters' pennies, alongside the comedians, clowns, freak shows, wild animals, monsters, giants, dwarfs, and the carnivalesque performances like rope-dancing and fire-eating. Now and again the university authorities attempted to prohibit the performance of plays at the Sturbridge Fair, as in a 1592 decree that banned the performance of all plays within five miles of Cambridge. A royal charter granted in the early 1600s gave the university vice chancellor powers to "prohibit idle games and diversions" and to "expel jugglers and actors." But like most laws, it was poorly policed and largely ineffective. By the end of the eighteenth century, every year the fair sported two theaters. John Gay's *The Beggar's Opera* was performed there in 1767.

The Oyster House was a public house built on Garlic Row in the years when the temporary rows of the fair had become streets with permanent buildings. In later years, when the fair was in its decline, the Oyster House became the center of activities for carousing, with local musicians playing for dancing on the upper floor. The fair went into terminal decline after World War I, but the Oyster House and the nearby Dog and Pheasant pub remained places where those who did attend the fair could be entertained by the musicians. In 1933 the depleted fair was opened officially for the final time, and it was abolished legally in 1934 by an order of the secretary of state. The last musicians to play in the Oyster House at fair time were Charlie Huntlea, Harry Day, and Herb Reynolds. Fortunately, some of the tunes they played there are known and included in the set list on page 143. One of the favorite tunes played and sung at the Oyster House was "We Won't Go Home Till Morning," of which only the second verse is commonly sung as "For He's a Jolly Good Fellow."

The Oyster House closed in 1957 and remained derelict until it was demolished in 1960. Workmen demolishing the building discovered huge tanks in the basement where in former years live oysters had been kept during the fair. They were smashed to pieces, and nothing remains of the building where over so many years so many people had a good time. It was not considered to be an historic monument. The last vestiges of the fair were suppressed in 1969, when rubble was dumped across the entrances to the common by order of the city council to keep out travelers, who until then had continued to visit Sturbridge Common annually at fair time after the official discontinuance of the fair in 1934.

The Oyster House Project was set up to encourage people to play and perform those tunes known to have been played in the last years of the fair. The songs are important because as a group of tunes they are part of historic Cambridge tradition, defining, in part, a local identity. When we play them mindful of their history at the Oyster House, we recall the magic that they wrought on others, long dead. Following is a list of tunes played at the Oyster House, Cambridge, in the late nineteenth to the early twentieth centuries, compiled from archival material by Nigel Campbell Pennick, 2009–2011.

"Soldier's Joy"
"The Girl I Left Behind Me"
"Smash the Windows"
"Birds-a-Building"
"Flowers of Edinburgh"
"Dumfries House"
"The Gay Gordons"
"Chaff and Cuttings"
"Dark-Eyed Sailor"
"Cock o' the North"
"Washington Post"
"Post-Horn Gallop"
"Liberty Bell"
"Under the Double Eagle"
"The Belphegorian March"
"Shave the Fiddle"
"The Triumph"
"Pop Goes the Weasel"
"We Won't Go Home Till Morning"

"Double Change Sides"
"The Keel Row"
"The Rose Tree"
"Bob Ridley-O (Shave the Donkey)"
"Gypsies in the Wood"
"The Sailors' Hornpipe (Ploughjack)"
"Cross-Hand Polka"
"Broom Dance Tune"
"All Jolly Fellows That Follows the Plough"
"The Cambridge Hornpipe"

BIBLIOGRAPHY

Abercrombie, Patrick. 1933. *Town and Country Planning.* London: Thornton Butterworth.

Ackerman, Hans-W., and Jean Gauthier. 1991. "The Ways and Nature of the Zombi." *Journal of American Folklore* 104, no. 414 (Autumn): 466–94.

Ackerman, John Yonge. 1885. *Remains of Pagan Saxondom.* London: John Russell Smith.

Ackroyd, Peter. 1990. *Dickens.* London: Vintage.

Adams, W. H. Davenport. 1895. *Witch, Warlock, and Magician: Historical Sketches of Magic and Witchcraft in England and Scotland.* London: Chatto & Windus.

Addison, Joseph. 1712. *Spectator* 414 (June 25), 101–2.

Addison, William. 1953. *English Fairs and Markets.* London: Batsford.

Agrippa, Heinrich Cornelius. 1651. *Three Books of Occult Philosophy.* Translated by James Freake. London: n.p.

Aitkin, Don. 1990. "20 Years of Festivals in Britain." *Festival Eye:* 18–21.

Andrews, William. 1890. *Curiosities of the Church: Studies of Curious Customs, Services, and Records.* London: Methuen.

———, ed. 1891. *Old Church Lore.* London: William Andrews.

———, ed. 1899. *Ecclesiastical Curiosities.* London: William Andrews.

Anonymous. 2006. *Conjuration and an Excellent Discourse of the Nature and Substance of Devils and Spirits in Two Books.* Hinckley, England: Society of Esoteric Endeavour.

Appel, W. 1951. "The Kentford Grave." *East Anglian Magazine,* June, 615–16.

Ash, Amin, ed. 1994. *Post-Fordism: A Reader.* Oxford, England: Blackwell.

Ashton, John. 1896. *The Devil in Britain and America.* London: Ward and Downing.

Aslet, Clive. 1997. *Anyone for England? A Search for British Identity*. London: Little, Brown.

Bächtold-Stäubli, Hanns, ed. 1927–1942. *Handwörterbuch des Deutschen Aberglaubens*. 9 vols. Berlin: Koehler und Amerlang.

Baillie Scott, Mackay Hugh. 1906. *Houses and Gardens*. London: George Newnes.

———. 1909. "Ideals in Buildings, False and True." In *The Arts Connected with Building*, edited by R. Weir Schulz. London: Batsford.

Bakhtin, M. 1984. *Rabelais and His World*. Bloomington: Indiana University Press.

Bales, E. G. 1939. "Folklore from West Norfolk." *Folklore* 50, no. 1 (March): 66–75.

Barnes, Richard, ed. 1983. *The Sun in the East: Norfolk & Suffolk Fairs*. Kirstead, England: RB Photographic.

Barrell, John. 1980. *The Dark Side of the Landscape*. Cambridge, England: Cambridge University Press.

Barthes, Roland. 1973. *Mythologies*. London: Paladin.

Baudrillard, Jean. 1981. *For a Critique of the Political Economy of the Sign*. Translated by Charles Levin. St. Louis, Mo.: Telos Press.

Bauman, Zygmunt. 1987. *Legislators and Interpreters: On Modernity, Postmodernity, and Intellectuals*. Cambridge, England: Polity Press.

Behrend, Michael. 1975. *The Landscape Geometry of Southern Britain*. Bar Hill, England: Institute of Geomantic Research.

Bell, Quentin. 1948. *On Human Finery*. London: Hogarth Press.

Bender, Barbara, ed. 1993. *Landscape: Politics and Perspectives*. Oxford, England: Berg.

Blain, Jenny, and Robert J. Wallis. 2002. "A Living Landscape? Pagans, Archaeology, and Spirits in the Land." *3rd Stone: Archaeology, Folklore, and Myth—The Magazine for the New Anitquarian* 43 (Summer): 20–27.

Blanchot, Maurice. 1993. *The Infinite Conversation*. Translated by Susan Hanson. Minneapolis: University of Minnesota Press.

Borst, Lyle B., and Barbara M. Borst. 1975. *Megalithic Software: Part I; England*. Williamsville, N.Y.: Twin Bridge Press.

Bottrell, William. 1880. *Stories and Folk-Lore of West Cornwall*. Penzance, England: F. Rodda.

Boyes, Georgina. 1993. *The Imagined Village: Culture, Ideology, and the English Folk Revival*. Manchester, England: Manchester University Press.

Braekman, Willy Louis. 1997. *Middeleeuwse witte en zwarte magie in het Nederlands taalgebied.* Ghent, Belgium: Koninklijke Academie voor Nederlandse Taal-en Letterkunde.

Bragdon, Claude. 1913. *Projective Ornament.* Rochester, N.Y.: Manas Press.

Brearley, R. 1951. "The Kentford Grave." *East Anglian Magazine,* August, 7–20.

Briggs, Katharine Mary. 1962. *Pale Hecate's Team.* London: Routledge & Kegan Paul.

Brill, Edith. 1990. *Life and Traditions on the Cotswolds.* Stroud, England: Alan Sutton Publishing.

Brockie, William. 1886. *Legends and Superstitions of the County of Durham.* Sunderland, England: B. Williams.

Bronner, Simon J. 1992. *Creativity and Tradition in Folklore: New Directions.* Logan: Utah State University Press.

Brooke, Rupert. 1949. *The Collected Poems of Rupert Brooke.* London: Medici Society.

Brown, Stuart J. 1982. *Albion and Crossley Buses in Camera.* Shepperton, England: Ian Allan.

Brown, Theo. 1958. "The Black Dog." *Folklore* 69 (September): 175–92.

———. 1962. "The Dartmoor Entrance to the Underworld." *Devon and Cornwall Notes and Queries* XXIX: 6–7.

———. 1966. "The Triple Gateway." *Folklore* 77: 123–31.

———. 1970. "Charming in Devon." *Folklore* 81: 37–47.

Browne, Sylvia. 2007. *Secret Societies . . . and How They Affect Our Lives Today.* New Delhi: Hay House.

Bunn, Ivan. 1977a. "Black Shuck. Part One: Encounters, Legends, and Ambiguities." *Lantern* 18 (Summer): 3–6.

———. 1977b. "Black Shuck. Part Two." *Lantern* 19 (Autumn): 4–8.

———. 1982. "A Devil's Shield: Notes on Suffolk Witch Bottles." *Lantern* 39 (Autumn): 3–7.

Burgess, Michael W. 1978. "Crossroad and Roadside Burials." *Lantern* 24 (Autumn): 6–8.

Burn, Ronald. 1914. "Folk-Lore from Newmarket, Cambridgeshire." *Folk-Lore* 25, no. 3 (September): 363–66.

Burne, Charlotte Sophia, and Georgina Frederica Jackson. 1883. *Shropshire Folk-Lore.* London: Trübner & Co.

Burns, Robert G. H. 2007. "Continuity, Variation, and Authenticity in the English Folk-Rock Movement." *Folk Music Journal* 9, no. 1: 192–218.

Burridge, Frank. 1975. *Nameplates of the Big Four.* Oxford: Oxford Publishing Company.

Canney, Maurice A. 1926. "The Use of Sand in Magic and Religion." *Man* (January): 13.

Carpenter, Edward. 1912. *The Art of Creation: Essays on the Self and Its Powers.* London: George Allan.

Carr-Gomm, Philip, and Richard Heygate. 2010. *The Book of English Magic.* London: John Murray.

Chambers, Sir William. 1772. *A Dissertation on Oriental Gardening.* London: W. Griffin.

Chetwynd-Stapylton, Mark. 1968. *Discovering Wayside Graves and Memorial Stones.* Tring, England: Shire Publications.

Chin Kung. 2004. *Changing Destiny: A Commentary on Liofan's Four Lessons.* Taipei, Taiwan: Corporation Republic of Hwa Dzan Society.

Chippindale, Christopher. 1987. *Stonehenge Complete.* London: Thames & Hudson.

Chippindale, Christopher, Paul Devereux, Rhys Jones, and Tim Sebastian, eds. 1990. *Who Owns Stonehenge?* London: Batsford.

Chomsky, Noam. 1977. "Objectivity and Liberal Scholarship." *Cienfuegos Press Anarchist Review* 1, no. 3 (Autumn): 38–58.

Chumbley, Andrew. 2000. *Grimoire of the Golden Toad.* London: Xoanon Publishing.

Clark, H. F. 1962. "The Mandrake Fiend." *Folklore* 73, no. 4 (Winter): 257–69.

Clarke, Michael. 1982. *The Politics of Pop Festivals.* London: Junction Books.

Clarke, W. G. 1925. *In Breckland Wilds.* London: Robert Scott.

Cloke, Paul, and Jo Little, eds. 1997. *Contested Countryside Cultures: Otherness, Marginalization, and Rurality.* London: Routledge.

Cohen, Erick, Nachman Ben-Yahuda, and Janet Aviad. 1987. "Recentering the World: The Quest for 'Elective' Centers in a Secularized Universe." *Sociological Review* 35, no. 2 (May): 320–46.

Constantine, Mary-Ann, and Gerald Porter. 2003. *Fragments and Meaning in Traditional Songs: From the Blues to the Baltic.* Oxford, England: Oxford University Press for the British Academy.

Conway, Moncure Daniel. 1879. *Demonology and Devil-Lore.* London: Ballantyne, Hanson, and Co.

Cooke, Grace, and Ivan Cooke. 1971. *The Light in Britain.* London: White Eagle Lodge.

Coombs, Rose E. 1983. *Before Endeavours Fade: A Guide to the Battlefields of the First World War.* London: Battle of Britain Prints International.

Coulter-Smith, Graham. 2002. *The Postmodern Art of Imants Tillers: Appropriation en abyme, 1971–2001.* Southampton: Southampton Institute and Paul Holberton Publishing.

Craigie, William Alexander. 1896. *Scandinavian Folk-Lore.* London: Paisley.

Crimp, Douglas. 1985. "On the Museum's Ruins." In *Postmodern Culture,* edited by Hal Foster, 43–56. London: Pluto Press.

Croft, D. G. 1971. "Linking Leys and UFOs." *Ley Hunter* 21.

Crooke, W. 1909. "Burial of Suicides at Crossroads." *Folklore* 20: 88–89.

Dalton, Michael. 1618. *The Country Justice.* London: Society of Stationers.

Dalyell, John Graham. 1834. *The Darker Superstitions of Scotland.* Edinburgh: Waugh & Innes.

Danser, Simon. 2005. *The Myths of Reality.* Wymeswold, England: Alternative Albion.

Davidson, Thomas. 1956. "The Horseman's Word: A Rural Initiation Ceremony." *Gwerin* 1, issue 2: 67–74.

Davies, Jonathan Ceredig. 1908. "Ghost-Raising in Wales." *Folklore* 19, no. 3 (September): 327–31.

Debord, Guy. 1994. *The Society of the Spectacle.* Translated by Donald Nicholson-Smith. New York: Zone Books.

Dégh, Linda. 1994. *American Folklore and the Mass Media.* South Bend: Indiana University Press.

Denham, Michael Aislabie. 1892. *The Denham Tracts.* London: David Nutt. Reprinted from the original tracts and pamphlets printed by Denham between 1846 and 1859.

Dickens, A. G. 1951. *The Register or Chronicle of Butley Priory, Suffolk, 1510–1535.* Winchester, England: Warren and Son.

Ditchfield, Peter Hampson. 1896. *Old English Customs Extant at the Present Time: An Account of Local Observances, Festival Customs, and Ancient Ceremonies Surviving in Great Britain.* London: Methuen.

Drake, Mavis R. 1989. *A Potpourri of East Anglian Witchcraft.* Royston: Sylvana Publications.

Drake-Carnell, Francis John. 1938. *Old English Ceremonies and Customs.* London: Batsford.

Dyer, T. F. Thistleton. 1878. *English Folk-Lore.* London: Bogue.

———. 1881. *Domestic Folk-Lore.* London: Cassell.

Eddrup, Rev. Canon. 1885. "Notes on Some Wiltshire Superstitions." *Wiltshire Archaeological and Natural History Magazine* 22: 330–34.

Egidius. 1935. "Magic in Norfolk." *East Anglian Magazine* 1, no. 2 (August): 93–95.

Eitel, Ernest John. 1873. *Feng-Shui, or the Rudiments of Natural Science in China.* London: Trübner & Co.

Elkins, James. 1992. "On Visual Desperation and the Bodies of Protozoa." *Representations* 40 (Autumn): 33–56.

Ellis-Davidson, Hilda. 1993. *The Lost Beliefs of Northern Europe.* London: Routledge.

Ericson, E. E. 1936. "Burial at the Cross-Roads." *Folklore* 47, no. 4: 374–75.

Ettlinger, Ellen. 1943. "Documents of British Superstition in Oxford." *Folklore* 54, no. 1 (March): 227–49.

Evans, George Ewart. 1971. *The Pattern under the Plough.* London: Faber and Faber.

Evans-Wentz, Walter Yeeling. 1911. *The Fairy Faith in Celtic Countries.* London: Oxford University Press.

Fanon, Frantz. 1952. *Peau noire, masques blancs.* Paris: Editions du Seuil.

Farrar, Stuart. 1972. *What Witches Do.* London: Peter Davies.

Flowers, Stephen. 1989. *The Galdrabók: An Icelandic Grimoire.* York Beach, Maine: Samuel Weiser.

Forman, Joan. 1974. *Haunted East Anglia.* London: Hale.

Forrest, Robert. 1976. "The Mathematical Case against Ley Lines and Related Topics." *Journal of Geomancy* 1, no. 1 (October): 10–15.

Foster, Hal. 2002. *Design and Crime (and Other Diatribes).* London and New York: Verso.

Foucault, Michel. 1976. *The Archaeology of Knowledge.* New York: Harper.

Franklin, Anna. 2002a. *The Illustrated Encyclopaedia of Fairies.* London: Vega.

———. 2002b. *Midsummer: Magical Celebrations of the Summer Solstice.* St. Paul, Minn.: Llewellyn.

Franklin, Anna, and Paul Mason. 2001. *Lammas: Celebrating the Fruits of the First Harvest.* St. Paul, Minn.: Llewellyn.

Franklin, Anna, with Paul Mason. 2010. *Lughnasa: History, Lore, and Celebration.* Earl Shilton, England: Lear Books.

Garrard, Bruce, Rainbow Jo, and Alistair McKay, eds. 1986. *Rainbow Village on the Road.* Glastonbury, England: Unique Publications.

Gerish, William Blyth. 1892. *Norfolk Folk-Lore.* London: Folk-Lore Society.

———. 1895. "A Churchyard Charm." *Folk-Lore* 6, no. 2 (June): 200.

———. 1911. *The Folk-Lore of Hertfordshire*. Hertfordshire: Bishop's Stortford.

Gilbert, William. 1911. "Witchcraft in Essex." *Transactions of the Essex Archaeological Society*, n.s., XI: 210–18.

Gill, W. W. 1944. "The One-Night House." *Folklore* 55, no. 3 (September): 128–32.

Girard, René. 1979. *Violence and the Sacred*. Baltimore, Md.: Johns Hopkins University Press.

Glyde, John, Jr. 1872. *Norfolk Garland: A Collection of the Superstitious Beliefs and Practices, Proverbs, Curious Customs, Ballads, and Songs of the People of Norfolk, as well as Anecdotes Illustrative of the Genius or Peculiarities of Norfolk Celebrities*. Norwich, England: Jarrold and Sons. Excerpted from *A New Suffolk Garland*, published in 1866.

———. 1976. *Folklore and Customs of Suffolk (A New Suffolk Garland, 1866)*. Norwich, England: EDP Publishing.

Goddard, Jimmy. 1966. "The Great Isosceles Triangle of England." *UFO Magazine* (Summer).

———. 1970. "Stone Circles and Patterns of Power." *Ley Hunter* 12.

———. 1971. "Unusual Trees—Symbols of Ley Power?" *Ley Hunter* 23.

Golding, John. 2000. *Paths to the Absolute*. London and New York: Thames & Hudson.

Golvers, Noël. 1994. "De recuiteringstocht van M. Martini, S.J. door de Lage Landen in 1654 over Geomantische Kompassen, Chinese verzamelingen, lichtbeelden en R.P. Wilhelm van Aelst, S.J." *De Zeventiende Eeuw* 10: 331–50.

Green, D. H. 2000. *Language and History in the Early Germanic World*. Cambridge, England: Cambridge University Press.

Gregor, Walter. 1881. *Notes on the Folk-Lore of the North-East of Scotland*. London: Folk-Lore Society.

Groves, Derham. 1991. *Feng-Shui and Western Building Ceremonies*. Lutterworth, England: Graham Brash, Singapore and Tynron Press.

Guidon. 2011. *Magic Secrets*. Translated by Philippe Pissier. Hinckley, England: Society of Esoteric Endeavour.

Gurdon, Camilla. 1892. "Folk-Lore from South-East Suffolk." *Folk-Lore* 3, no. 4 (December): 558–60.

Gurdon, Lady Evelyne C. 1893. *County Folk-Lore of Suffolk*. London: David Butt.

Gutch, Mrs., and Mabel Peacock. 1908. *Examples of Printed Folk-Lore Concerning Lincolnshire*. London: David Nutt.

Hadow, Grace E., and Ruth Anderson. 1924. "Scraps of English Folk-Lore IX (Suffolk)." *Folk-Lore* 35, no. 4 (December): 346–60.

Halfacre, K. H. 1993. "Locality and Social Representation: Space, Discourse, and Alternative Definitions of the Rural." *Journal of Rural Studies* 11, no. 1 (January): 23–37.

Hall, Stuart, and Tony Jefferson, eds. 1976. *Resistance through Ritual: Youth Subcultures in Post-War Britain.* London: Hutchinson/Centre for Contemporary Cultural Studies.

Halliday, Robert. 2010. "The Roadside Burial of Suicides: An East Anglian Study." *Folklore* 121, no. 1 (April): 81–93.

Harper, Charles G. 1904. *The Newmarket, Bury, Thetford, and Cromer Road.* London: Chapman and Hall.

Harrison, William. 1968. *The Description of England.* Edited by Georges Edelen. New York: Dover.

Harte, Jeremy. 1999. *Research in Geomancy 1990–1994: Readings in Sacred Space.* Wymeswold, England: Heart of Albion.

Hartley, Christine. 1968. *The Western Mystery Tradition.* London: Aquarian Press.

Hasenfratz, Hans-Peter. 2011. *Barbarian Rites: The Spiritual World of the Vikings and the Germanic Tribes.* Translated by Michael Moynihan. Rochester, Vt.: Inner Traditions.

Hawker, Robert Stephen. 1870. *Footprints of Former Men in Far Cornwall.* London: John Russell Smith.

Haynes, Edmund Sidney Pollack. 1906. *Religious Persecution: A Study in Political Psychology.* London: Watts.

Heanley, Rev. R. M. 1902. "The Vikings: Traces of their Folklore in Marshland." In *Saga-Book of the Viking Club,* 35–62. Vol. 3, part 1. London: privately printed.

Heelas, Paul. 1996. *The New Age Movement.* Oxford, England: Blackwell.

Heidegger, Martin. 1970. *Hegel's Concept of Experience.* New York: Harper & Row.

———. 1977. *The Question Concerning Technology and Other Essays.* Translated by William Lovett. New York: Harper & Row.

Henderson, William. 1866. *Notes on the Folk-Lore of the Northern Counties of England and the Border.* London: Longmans, Green and Co.

Hetherington, Kevin. 2000. *New Age Travellers: Vanloads of Uproarious Humanity.* London and New York: Cassell.

Hewett, Sarah. 1900. *Nummits and Crummits: Devonshire Customs.* London: Thomas Burleigh.

Hewison, Robert. 1987. *The Heritage Industry.* London: Methuen.

Hiller, Susan. 1995. *After the Freud Museum.* London: Book Works.

Hobsbawm, Eric, and Terence Ranger, eds. 1983. *The Invention of Tradition.* Cambridge, England: Cambridge University Press.

Hodson, Geoffrey. 1925. *Fairies at Work and Play.* London: Theosophical Publishing House.

Hole, Christina. 1977. "Protective Symbols in the Home." In *Symbols of Power,* edited by H. R. Ellis-Davidson. London: Folklore Society.

Holt, M. 1951. "A Moulton Grave." *East Anglian Magazine,* February, 358.

Horne, M. A. C. 1987. *The Northern Line.* Finchley, England: Douglas Rose.

Hyatt, Harry Middleton. 1970–1978. *Hoodoo, Conjuration, Witchcraft, Rootwork.* 5 vols. Hannibal, Mo.: Memoirs of the Alma Egan Hyatt Foundation.

Jameson, Fredric. 1991. *Postmodernism, or the Cultural Logic of Late Capitalism.* Durham, N.C.: Duke University Press.

Jefferies, Richard. 1889. *Wild Life in a Southern Country.* London: Longmans, Green and Co.

Jekyll, Gertrude. 1904. *Old West Surrey.* London: Longmans, Green and Co.

Johnson, Walter. 1912. *Byways in Archaeology.* Cambridge, England: Cambridge University Press.

Jones, Prudence. 1982. "Eight and Nine: Sacred Numbers of Sun and Moon in the Pagan North." Fenris-Wolf Pagan Paper, no. 2. Bar Hill, England: Fenris-Wolf.

Jones, Prudence, and Nigel Pennick. 1995. *A History of Pagan Europe.* London: Routledge.

Jones-Baker, Doris. 1977. *The Folklore of Hertfordshire.* London: B. T. Batsford Ltd.

Joyce, Paul. 2002. *Hockney on Art: Conversations with Paul Joyce.* London: Little, Brown.

Jung, Carl G. 1972. *Synchronicity: An Acausal Connecting Principle.* London: Routledge & Kegan Paul.

Kearns, Rev. J. F. 2001. *Silpa Sastra.* Cambridge, England: Institute of Experimental Geomancy.

Keith, Michael, and Steve Pile, eds. 1993. *Place and the Politics of Identity.* London: Routledge.

Koop, Kenneth. 1946. *The Earliest Survey of Britain.* Cairo: n.p.

Larsen, Egon. 1971. *Strange Sects and Cults*. London: Arthur Barker.

Latham, Charlotte. 1878. "Some West Sussex Superstitions Lingering in 1868." *Folk-Lore Record* 1: 1–67.

Laurie, Peter. 1972. *Beneath the City Streets*. Harmondsworth, England: Penguin. Revised edition, London: Granada, 1979.

Lawrence, Robert Means. 1898. *The Magic of the Horse Shoe*. Boston and New York: Houghton Mifflin.

Leather, Ella Mary. 1912. *The Folk-Lore of Herefordshire*. Hereford, England: Jakeman and Carver; London: Sidgwick and Jackson.

———. 1914. "Foundation Sacrifice." *Folk-Lore* 24: 110.

Lee, Rev. Frederick George, ed. 1875. *Glimpses of the Supernatural*. 2 vols. London: Henry S. King and Co.

Lefebvre, Henri. 1991. *The Production of Space*. Oxford, England: Blackwell.

Legeza, Laszlo. 1975. *Tao Magi: The Secret Language of Diagrams and Calligraphy*. London: Thames & Hudson.

Letcher, Andy. 2001. "The Scouring of the Shire: Fairies, Trolls, and Pixies in Eco-Protest Culture." *Folklore* 112, no. 2 (October): 147–61.

Lethaby, William Richard. *Architecture, Mysticism, and Myth*. London: Percival, 1891.

Lethbridge, Thomas Charles. 1957. *Gogmagog: The Buried Gods*. London: Routledge & Kegan Paul.

Loewe, Michael, and Carmen Blacker, eds. 1981. *Divination and Oracles*. London: George Allen & Unwin.

MacDonald, Michael, and Terence R. Murphy. 1990. *Sleepless Souls: Suicide in Early Modern England*. Oxford: Clarendon Press.

Macdonald, Sharon, and Gordon Fyfe, eds. 1996. *Theorizing Museums*. Oxford, England: Blackwell.

MacPherson, Joseph McKenzie. 1929. *Primitive Beliefs in the North East of Scotland*. London: Longmans, Green and Co.

Mallien, Lara, and Johannes Heimrath, eds. 2008. *Was ist Geomantie? Die neue Beziehung zu unseren Heimatplaneten*. Klein-Jasedow, Germany: Drachen Verlag.

———. 2009. *Genius Loci: Der Geist von Orten und Lanschaften in Geomantie und Architektur*. Klein-Jasedow, Germany: Drachen Verlag.

Malraux, Andre. 1954. *The Voices of Silence*. London: Secker & Warburg.

March, H. Colley. 1899. "Dorset Folk-Lore Collected in 1897." *Folk-Lore* 10, no. 4 (December): 478–89.

Marquis, Amy. 2009. *Lumière: Lithographs by Odilon Redon.* Cambridge, England: Fitzwilliam Museum.

Matless, David. 1993. "Appropriate Geography: Patrick Abercrombie and the Energy of the World." *Journal of Design History* 6, no. 3 (September): 167–78.

McAldowie, Alex. 1896. "Personal Experiences in Witchcraft." *Folk-Lore* 7: 309–14.

McFadzean, Patrick. 1999. *Vastu Vidya: Studies in Indian Geomancy.* Cambridge: Institute of Experimental Geomancy.

McNeill, F. Marian. 1957–1968. *The Silver Bough.* 4 vols. Glasgow, Scotland: William Maclellan.

Michell, John. 1967. *The Flying Saucer Vision.* London: Sidgwick & Jackson.

———. 1969. *The View over Atlantis.* London: Garnstone Press.

———. 1983. *The New View over Atlantis.* London: Thames & Hudson.

———. 1986. *Stonehenge: Its History, Meaning, Festival, Police Riot '85, and Future Prospects.* London: Radical Traditionalist Papers.

Mollet, Le Baron. 1947. "Les Origines du cubisme: Apollinaire, Picasso et Cie." *Les Lettres Françaises,* January: 3.

Monger, George. 1997. "Modern Wayside Shrines." *Folklore* 108: 113–15.

Mortimer, Bishop Robert. 1972. *Exorcism. The Findings of a Commission Convened by the Bishop of Exeter.* Edited by Dom Robert Petitpierre. London: Society for Promoting Christian Knowledge.

Neat, Timothy. 2002. *The Horseman's Word.* Edinburgh: Birlinn.

Newman, L. F., and E. M. Wilson. 1952. "Folklore Survivals in the Southern 'Lake Counties' and in Essex: A Comparison and Contrast." *Folklore* 63 (June): 91–104.

Newman, Leslie F. 1940. "Notes on Some Rural and Trade Initiations in the Eastern Counties." *Folklore* 51, no. 1 (March): 33–42.

———. 1946. "Some Notes on the Practice of Witchcraft in the Eastern Counties." *Folklore* 57, no. 1 (March): 12–32.

———. 1948a. "Some Notes on the Pharmacology and Therapeutic Value of Folk-Medicines I." *Folklore* 59, no. 3 (September): 118–35.

———. 1948b. "Some Notes on the Pharmacology and Therapeutic Value of Folk-Medicines II." *Folklore* 59, no. 4 (December): 145–56.

Olivier, Fernande. 1933. *Picasso et ses Amis.* Paris: Stock.

Palmer, Roy. 1992. *Folklore of Hereford and Worcester.* Woonton Almeley, England: Logaston Press.

———. 2004. *The Folklore of Shropshire.* Woonton Almeley, England: Logaston Press.

Parker, Barry, and Raymond Unwin. 1901. *The Art of Building a Home.* New York, London, and Bombay: Longmans, Green and Co.

Parsons, Catherine E. 1915. "Notes on Cambridgeshire Witchcraft." *Proceedings of the Cambridge Antiquarian Society* XIX, LXVII: 31–52.

———. 1952. *Horseheath: Some Recollections of a Cambridgeshire Parish.* London: Little Abingdon.

Pattinson, G. W. 1953. "Adult Education and Folklore." *Folklore* 64, no. 3 (September): 424–26.

Paye, Peter. 2009. *The Wisbech & Upwell Tramway.* Usk, Wales: Oakwood Press.

Peacock, Mabel Geraldine W. 1896. "Executed Criminals and Folk Medicine." *Folk-Lore* 7, no. 3 (September): 268–83.

———. 1897. "Omens of Death." *Folk-Lore* 8: 377–78.

———. 1901. "The Folk-Lore of Lincolnshire." *Folk-Lore* 12: 161–80.

Peacock, Mabel Geraldine W., Katherine Carson, and Charlotte Burne. 1901. "Customs Relating to Iron." *Folk-Lore* 12, no. 4 (December): 472–75.

Pennant, Thomas. 1793. *The History of the Parishes of Whiteford and Holywell.* London: Benjamin & J. White.

Pennick, Nigel. 1979. *The Ancient Science of Geomancy: Man in Harmony with the Earth.* London: Thames & Hudson.

———. 1980. *Sacred Geometry: Symbolism and Purpose in Religious Structures.* Wellingborough, England: Aquarian Press.

———. 1985a. *The Cosmic Axis.* Bar Hill, England: Runestaff.

———. 1985b. *Daddy Witch and Old Mother Redcap.* Cambridge, England: Cornerstone Press.

———. 1985c. "Geomantic Reflections." *Practical Geomancy* 1, no. 1 (Winter): 13–14.

———. 1986. *Skulls, Cats, and Witch Bottle.* Bar Hill, England: Nigel Pennick Editions.

———. 1987a. "The Subterranean Kingdom. Part One: Secret Rites in Secret Places." *Supernatural* 1, no. 12 (July): 49–53.

———. 1987b. "The Subterranean Kingdom. Part Two: Darkness and Light." *Supernatural* 1, no. 13 (August): 33–37.

———. 1988. *Bunkers under London.* The Tube Railways of London Series, no. 2. Bar Hill, England: Valknut Productions.

———. 1989. *Practical Magic in the Northern Tradition.* Wellingborough, England: Thorsons.

———. 1992a. *The Pagan Source Book: A Guide to Festivals, Traditions, and Symbols of the Year.* London: Rider.

———. 1992b. "The Reality Censors: The World as Real Estate." *Fortean Times* 62 (April): 45–46.

———. 1995. *Secrets of East Anglian Magic.* London: Robert Hale, 1995. 2nd edition, Milverton, England: Capall Bann Publishing, 2004.

———. 1996. *Celtic Sacred Landscapes.* London and New York: Thames & Hudson.

———. 1997. *Leylines.* London: Wiedenfeld & Nicolson.

———. 1998. *Crossing the Borderlines: Guising, Masking, & Ritual Animal Disguises in the European Tradition.* Chieveley, England: Capall Bann Publishing.

———. 1999a. *Beginnings. Geomancy, Builders' Rites, and Electional Astrology in the European Tradition.* Chieveley, England: Capall Bann Publishing.

———. 1999b. "Regarding the Ooser." *3rd Stone* 35 (July–September): 39–40.

———. 2002. *The Power Within: The Way of the Warrior and the Martial Arts in the European Tradition.* Chieveley, England: Capall Bann Publishing.

———. 2003. "Postmoderne Monumente." *Hagia Chora* 17: 109.

———. 2003–2004. "Heathen Holy Places in Northern Europe: A Cultural Overview." *Tyr: Myth-Culture-Tradition* 2: 139–49.

———. 2004. *Threshhold and Hearthstone Patterns.* Bar Hill, England: Old England House.

———. 2005a. *Natural Magic.* Earl Shilton, England: Lear Books.

———. 2005b. *The Spiritual Arts and Crafts.* Bar Hill: Spiritual Arts & Crafts Publishing.

———. 2005c. "Vom Fortbestehen alter Grenzen." *Hagia Chora* 20: 103.

———. 2006a. *The Eldritch World.* Earl Shilton, England: Lear Books.

———. 2006b. *Folk-Lore of East Anglia and Adjoining Counties.* Bar Hill, England: Spiritual Arts & Crafts Publishing.

———. 2006c. *The Spiritual Arts and Crafts.* Barr Hill, England: Spiritual Arts & Crafts Publishing.

———. 2007. *Primal Signs: Traditional Glyphs and Symbols.* Bar Hill, England: Spiritual Arts & Crafts Publishing.

———. 2010a. "Pines on the Horizon, or, Seeing What We Want To See." *Silver Wheel Annual* 2: 97–101.

———. 2010b. *Wyrdstaves of the North.* Earl Shilton: Lear Books, 2010. Revised edition, *Runic Lore and Legend: Wyrdstaves of Old Northumbria,* Rochester, Vt.: Destiny Books, 2019.

———. 2011a. *In Field and Fen.* Earl Shilton, England: Lear Books, 2011. Revised edition, *Witchcraft & Secret Societies of Rural England,* Rochester, Vt.: Destiny Books, 2019.

———. 2011b. *Secrets of King's College Chapel.* London: Aeon.

———. 2011c. *The Toadman.* Hinckley, England: Society of Esoteric Endeavour.

Pennick, Nigel, and Paul Devereux. 1989. *Lines on the Landscape: Leys and Other Linear Enigmas.* London: Robert Hale.

Pennick, Nigel, and Helen Field. 2003. *A Book of Beasts.* Milverton, England: Capall Bann Publishing.

Petersson, Anna. 2009. "Swedish *Offerkast* and Recent Roadside Memorials." *Folklore* 120, no. 1 (April): 75–91.

Pittaway, Andy, and Bernard Scofield. 1976a. *Country Bazaar: A Handbook of Country Pleasures.* London: Fontana.

———. 1976b. *The Complete Country Bizarre.* London: Astragal.

Porteous, Crichton. 1976. *The Ancient Customs of Derbyshire.* Derby, England: Derbyshire Countryside.

Porter, Enid 1969. *Cambridgeshire Customs and Folklore.* London: Routledge & Kegan Paul. Fenland material provided by W. H. Barrett.

———. 1974. *The Folklore of East Anglia.* London: Batsford.

Puhvel, Martin. 1976. "The Mystery of the Cross-Roads." *Folklore* 87: 167–77.

Rafferty, Kevin, Jayne Loader, and Pierce Rafferty. 1982. *The Atomic Café.* New York: Peacock Press/Bantam.

Raine, James.1835. *Book of Depositions from 1565 to 1573.* Vol. XXI. London: Publications of the Surtees Society.

Randall, Arthur, and Enid Porter, eds. 1966. *Sixty Years a Fenman.* London: Routledge & Kegan Paul.

Rawlence, E. A. 1914. "Folk-Lore and Superstition Still Obtaining in Dorset." *Proceedings of the Dorsetshire Natural History and Antiquarian Field Club* 35: 81–87.

Rayson, George. 1865a. "East Anglian Folk-Lore, no. 1. 'Weather Proverbs.'" *East Anglian, or, Notes and Queries on Subjects Connected with the Counties of Suffolk, Cambridgeshire, Essex, and Norfolk* I: 155–62.

———. 1865b. "East Anglian Folk-Lore, no. 2. 'Omens.'" *East Anglian, or,*

Notes and Queries on Subjects Connected with the Counties of Suffolk, Cambridgeshire, Essex, and Norfolk I: 185–86.

———. 1865c. "East Anglian Folk-Lore, no. 3. 'Charms.'" *East Anglian, or, Notes and Queries on Subjects Connected with the Counties of Suffolk, Cambridgeshire, Essex, and Norfolk* I: 214–17.

Read, D. H. Moutray. 1911. "Hampshire Folk-Lore." *Folk-Lore* 22, no. 3 (September): 292–329.

Rees, Rev. R. Wilkins. 1898. "Ghost Laying." In *The Church Treasury of History, Custom, Folk-Lore etc.,* edited by William Andrews, 240–70. London: William Andrews.

Reeves, James, ed. 1958. *The Idiom of the People: English Traditional Verse, Edited with an Introduction and Notes from the Manuscripts of Cecil J. Sharp.* London: Heinemann.

Reichenbach, Baron C. 1926. *Letters on Od and Magnetism.* London: Hutchinson.

Renne, Elisha P. 1994. "Things That Threaten: A Symbolic Analysis of Bunu Yoruba Masquerades." *Res* 26 (Autumn): 100–112.

Rennie, William, et. al. 2009. *The Society of the Horseman's Word.* Hinckley, England: Society of Esoteric Endeavour.

Reuter, Otto Sigfrid. 1985. *Sky Lore of the North.* Translated by Michael Behrend. Bar Hill, Endland: Runestaff.

Riley, Bridget. 2009. *The Eye's Mind: Bridget Riley, Collected Writings 1965–2009.* Edited by Robert Kudielka. London: Thames & Hudson.

Roper, Charles. 1883. "On Witchcraft Superstition in Norfolk." *Harper's New Monthly Magazine* 87, no. 521 (October): 792–97.

Ross, Cathy. 2003. *Twenties London: A City in the Jazz Age.* London: Museum of London/Philip Wilson Publishers.

Rudkin, Ethel. 1933. "Lincolnshire Folk-Lore." *Folk-Lore* 44, no. 3 (September): 279–95.

———. 1934. "Lincolnshire Folk-Lore, Witches and Devils." *Folk-Lore* 45, no. 3 (September): 249—67.

———. 1936. *Lincolnshire Folklore.* Gainsborough, England: Beltons.

Russell, Jeffrey. 1972. *Witchcraft in the Middle Ages.* Ithaca, N.Y.: Cornell University Press.

Russett, Vince. 1978. "At the Gallows Pole." *Picwinnard* 7 (November): 15–20.

Sadler, Ida. 1962. "Fifty Years of Working with Horses." *Cambridgeshire Local History Council Bulletin* 18 (Summer): 10–16.

Said, Edward W. 1993. *Culture and Imperialism.* New York: Alfred A. Knopf.

Salmon, L. 1902. "Folk-Lore in the Kennet Valley." *Folk-Lore* 13, no. 4 (December): 418–29.

Samuel, Raphael, and Paul Thompson, eds. 1990. *The Myths We Live By.* London: Routledge.

Sartori, Paul. 1898. "Ueber das Bauopfer." *Zeitschrift für Ethnologie* 30: 1–54.

Sartre, Jean-Paul. 1948. *Black Orpheus.* Translated by S. W. Allen. Paris: Présence Africaine.

———. 1962. *Literary and Philosophical Essays.* Translated by S. W. Allen. New York: Collier.

Saunders, W. H. Bernard. 1888. *Legends and Traditions of Huntingdonshire.* London: Simpkin Marshall, Elliot Stock; and Huntington, England: Geo. C. Caster.

Schmalenbach, Herman. 1977. "Communion—A Sociological Category." In *Herman Schmalenbach: On Society and Experience,* edited by Günther Lüschen and Gregory Stone, 64–125. Chicago: University of Chicago Press.

Schroyer, Trent. 1973. *The Critique of Domination.* New York: George Braziller.

Scott, Sir Walter. 1885. *Letters on Demonology and Witchcraft.* 2nd ed. London and New York: George Routledge and Sons.

Screeton, Paul. 1974. *Quicksilver Heritage: The Mystic Leys—Their Legacy of Ancient Wisdom.* Wellingborough, England: Thorsons.

Seabrook, John. 2000. *Nobrow: The Culture of Marketing, the Marketing of Culture.* New York: Alfred A. Knopf.

Seymour, John D. 1913. *Irish Witchcraft and Demonology.* Dublin: Hodges Figgis.

Shoard, Marion. 1981. *The Theft of the Countryside.* London: Temple Smith.

Shuttlewood, Arthur. 1967. *The Warminster Mystery.* Sudbury, England: Neville Spearman.

Simper, Robert. 1980. *Traditions of East Anglia.* Woodbridge, England: Boydell Press.

Singer, William. 1881. *An Exposition of the Miller and Horseman's Word, or the True System of Raising the Devil.* Aberdeen, Scotland: James Daniel.

Sircello, Guy. 1990. "Beauty in Shards and Fragments." *Journal of Aesthetics and Art Criticism* 48, no. 1: 22–32.

Smith, A. W. 1966. "Some Folklore Elements in Movements of Social Protest." *Folklore* 77: 241–52.

Smith, Robert James. 1999. "Roadside Memorials—Some Australian Examples." *Folklore* 110: 103–4.

Speth, G. W. 1894. "Builders' Rites and Ceremonies." *Margate: Keeble's Gazette.*

Starsmore, Ian. 1975. *English Fairs.* London: Thames & Hudson.

Stedman-Jones, Gareth. 1983. *Languages of Class.* Cambridge, England: Cambridge University Press.

Steegmuller, Francis. 1963. *Apollinaire: Poet among the Painters.* London: Rupert Hart-Davis.

Sternberg, Thomas. 1851. *The Dialect and Folk-Lore of Northamptonshire.* London: John Russell Smith; Northampton, England: Abel & Sons, G. N. Wetton; Oundle, England: R. Todd; and Brackley, England: A. Green.

Stone, Alby. 1998. *Straight Track, Crooked Road: Leys, Spirit Paths, and Shamanism.* Wymeswold, England: Heart of Albion Press.

Stone, Christopher James. 1996. *Fierce Dancing.* London: Faber and Faber.

Strachan, Gordon. 2003. *Chartres: Sacred Geometry, Sacred Space.* Edinburgh: Floris Books.

Strathern, Marilyn. 1992. *After Nature.* Cambridge, England: Cambridge University Press.

Stretton, Clement E. 1909. *Tectonic Art: Ancient Trade Guilds and Companies.* Melton Mowbray, England: Melton Mowbray Times Company.

Ström, Ake V. 1975. "Germanische Religion." *Die Religion Der Menschheit* 19, part I. Stuttgart, Germany: Kohlhammer.

Tacitus. 1959. *Germania.* Edited by Manfred Fuhrmann. Stuttgart, Germany: Reclam.

Taussig, Michael. 1993. *Mimesis and Alterity: A Particular History of the Senses.* London: Routledge.

Taylor, Isaac. *Notes & Queries.* 9th series, iv, 335.

Taylor, Mark R. 1929. "Norfolk Folk-Lore." *Folk-Lore* 40, no. 2 (June): 113–33.

Tebbutt, C. F. 1942. "Huntingdonshire Folk and their Folklore." *Transactions of the Cambridgeshire and Huntingdonshire Archaeological Society* VI: 119–54.

———. 1950. "Huntingdonshire Folk and their Folklore." *Transactions of the Cambridgeshire and Huntingdonshire Archaeological Society* VII: 54–64.

———. 1984. *Huntingdonshire Folklore.* St. Ives, England: Norris Museum.

Temple, Sir William. 1685. *Upon the Gardens of Epicurus.* London: Chatto & Windus.

Trevelyan, Marie. 1909. *Folk-Lore and Folk Stories of Wales.* London: E. Stock.

Trubshaw, Bob. 1995. "The Metaphors and Rituals of Place and Time. An Introduction to Liminality." *Mercian Mysteries* 22 (February): 1–8.

———. 2005. *Sacred Places, Prehistory, and Popular Imagination.* Wymeswold, England: Heart of Albion Press.

Turner, Victor. 1973. "The Center Out There: Pilgrim's Goal." *History of Religion* 12, no. 3: 191–230.

Tyack, George S. 1899. *Lore and Legend of the English Church.* London: William Andrews.

Urry, John. 1990. *The Tourist Gaze: Leisure and Travel in Contemporary Societies.* London: Sage.

Valiente, Doreen. 1984. *An ABC of Witchcraft Past and Present.* London: Hale.

Van Duyn, Roel. 1972. *Message of a Wise Kabouter.* Translated by Hubert Hoskins. London: Duckworth.

Vaneigem, Raoul. 1975. *The Revolution of Everyday Life.* London: Practical Paradise.

Veblen, Thorstein Bunde. 1973. *The Theory of the Leisure Class: An Economic Study of Institutions.* Boston, Mass.: Houghton Mifflin.

von Poseck, Helena. 1905. "How John Chinaman Builds His House." *East of Asia Magazine.* Reprinted September 1979 as *Feng-Shui and the Chinese House.* Cambridge, England: Institute of Geomantic Research Occasional Paper, no. 14.

Ward Williams, Howard. 1865. *The Superstitions of Witchcraft.* London: Longman, Roberts and Green.

Warren, Adrian, and Dale Sasitorn. 2005. *England: The Mini-Book of Aerial Views.* Panborough, England: Last Refuge Ltd.

Webb, Denzil. 1969. "Irish Charms in Northern England." *Folklore* 80: 262–65.

Webb, James. 1974. *The Occult Underground.* La Salle, Ill.: Open Court.

Weber, Max. 1985. *The Protestant Ethic and the Spirit of Capitalism.* London: Counterpoint/Unwin.

Webster, David, ed. 1820. *Collection of Rare and Curious Tracts on Witchcraft.* Edinburgh: T. Webster.

Weever, John. 1631. *Ancient Funerall Monuments.* London: Thomas Harper.

Werbner, Richard. 1989. *Ritual Passage, Sacred Journey.* Manchester, England: Manchester University Press.

Wheeler, William Henry. 1868. *History of the Fens of South Lincolnshire.* Boston, Mass.: J. M. Newcomb; and London: Simpkin, Marshall & Co.

White, Hayden. 1973. *Metahistory: The Historical Imagination in Nineteenth Century Europe.* Baltimore, Md.: Johns Hopkins University Press.

Wildman, Sam G. 1971. *The Black Horsemen.* London: Garnstone Press.

Williams-Ellis, Clough. 1928. *England and the Octopus.* London: Geoffrey Bles.

Wood-Martin, William Gregory. 1902. *Traces of the Elder Faith of Ireland.* 2 vols. London: Longmans, Green and Co.

Wright, Arthur R. 1912. "Seventeenth Century Cures and Charms." *Folk-Lore* 23, no. 2 (June): 230–36.

Wright, Arthur R., and T. E. Lones. 1936. *British Calendar Customs I. Movable Festivals.* London: William Glaisher Ltd.

———. 1938. *British Calendar Customs II. Fixed Festivals, January–May, Inclusive.* London: William Glaisher Ltd.

———. 1940. *British Calendar Customs III. Fixed Festivals, June–December, Inclusive.* London: William Glaisher Ltd.

Wright, Arthur R., and W. Aldis Wright. 1912. "Seventeenth Century Cures and Charms." *Folk-Lore* 23, no. 4 (December): 490–97.

Wright, Patrick. 1985. *On Living in an Old Country.* London: Verso.

Wykes, Alan. 1979. *Ale and Hearty: Gleanings from the History of Brews and Brewing.* London: Jupiter Books.

INDEX

Page numbers in *italics* indicate illustrations

Books of Related Interest

Runic Lore and Legend
Wyrdstaves of Old Northumbria
by Nigel Pennick

Pagan Magic of the Northern Tradition
Customs, Rites, and Ceremonies
by Nigel Pennick

The Pagan Book of Days
A Guide to the Festivals, Traditions, and Sacred Days of the Year
by Nigel Pennick

The Book of Primal Signs
The High Magic of Symbols
by Nigel Pennick

Runic Book of Days
A Guide to Living the Annual Cycle of Rune Magick
by S. Kelley Harrell
Foreword by Nigel Pennick

How the World Is Made
The Story of Creation according to Sacred Geometry
by John Michell with Allan Brown

Nordic Runes
Understanding, Casting, and Interpreting the Ancient Viking Oracle
by Paul Rhys Mountfort

Spirits in Stone
The Secrets of Megalithic America
by Glenn Kreisberg
Foreword by Graham Hancock

INNER TRADITIONS • BEAR & COMPANY
P.O. Box 388
Rochester, VT 05767
1-800-246-8648
www.InnerTraditions.com

Or contact your local bookseller